What Is SEO – Search Engine Optimization 101

By:

Dan Kerns

License Notes

In our digitally dominated world, it is unusual for a business not to have an official website.

Just like employers now admit to avoiding job candidates without a Facebook presence, consumers have become distrustful of companies that they cannot find online [1]. It is why, every year, brands spend thousands of dollars on digital marketing [2].

Yet, it is not enough to just have a website. To drive traffic and keep visitor numbers high, it needs to be visible.

This is where things get difficult, because capturing the attention of internet users means competing for and achieving a top spot on the search engine results pages.

SEO is just the word used to describe these efforts to become more visible [3]. Some methods are easy, and others are harder to master.

With anywhere between 12 and 24 million businesses now selling products online, it would be impossible to find an audience without SEO [4].

So, the question is, how do internet users get to the content that they need? Specifically, how does a person go from entering a keyword into Google to making a purchase from just one of these businesses?

It all comes back to search engine optimization. It is the key to creating and maintaining a visible online presence.

What Is Search Engine Optimization?

The common mistake made with SEO is to confuse techniques with objectives.

There are several different ways to increase onpage SEO and incorporate it into online content.

However, they all amount to the same thing, even though they take different paths to get there. For a search engine to have any value, it must be able to quickly (usually, in an instant) order all of the results produced by a specific search [5].

For instance, imagine searching the word 'ice cream' in Google.

The job of the search engine is to return as many relevant results as possible; this means any web content which contains the word.

Clearly, this is going to amount to millions of webpages, and a good portion of them will not be useful. If a person is searching for food, then things like artwork, song titles, brand names, color palettes, and graphic designs are not helpful.

It is why Google arranges its results in order of relevance to the search term itself. In other words, food related content gets prioritized above everything else unless a more detailed description is given (for instance, 'ice cream song lyrics' or 'ice cream sneakers').

The problem is that this still leaves millions of pages to choose from, so layer upon layer of filters are added to continue narrowing the content [6].

These filters are broad ranging, and they turn search engines into a kind of police force for online content.

To make it through the filters and secure the most visible spot, businesses have to create content which pleases search engine algorithms.

It is achieved by convincing the algorithm that they are exactly what the original keyword was meant to find. For ice cream vendors in Denver, it is a fight to be more relevant than all the other ice cream vendors in Denver.

This is search engine optimization in its most basic form.

If a business pleases Google, it wins points.

The content gets pushed to the top of the search page, where it is easier to see.

Conversely, some actions can get content pushed back down the page. For example, letting web pages go stale, using broken links, and having a poor website design are all things that Google does not like [7]. They suggest that not enough care has been taken over the content and that it is not good enough for users.

Ultimately, it is about following the rules set out by Google and its online 'police force.' The more skillfully a company can do this, the better the outcome. It can be tricky at first, but great SEO comes with practice.

After enough time, it becomes second nature, and talented content developers can use key techniques without barely any effort at all.

For beginners and new companies, the advice is to start out small and master some basic onpage SEO before moving onto the harder methods.

What Is the Difference Between Onpage and Offpage SEO?

Search engine optimization is split into two categories; offpage and onpage.

They both have the same overall objective – greater visibility, so that more traffic can find the website. The difference between the two is very simple.

Offpage SEO involves external strategies. These are methods which focus on bringing value to the content from outside [8]. For instance, posting links and information about a website on social media platforms is a form of offpage SEO.

In contrast, onpage SEO involves changes made directly to the content, rather than external attempts to draw attention to it [9]. They are both valid ways to build up an online presence, but onpage SEO is more valuable because it offers a much greater degree of control.

The amount of influence over external content is limited. For every twenty links left on a Facebook page, only two might lead to any interest. It relies too heavily on the actions of others.

On-page SEO, on the other hand, is all about care and precision.

There is an extensive list of small (and bigger) changes which can be used to push content up on the search results pages [10]. They are much simpler to wield because they may be checked off a list.

Plus, they are almost impossible to get wrong once you know the rules.

One thing to remember is that the search engine algorithms which judge and review SEO are intelligent. They are extremely sophisticated and subject to constant scrutiny. Google has a reputation for updating its algorithms without warning, and it does this to keep standards high [11].

It means that every year, it gets easier to identify content which is, technically, following the rules but still offering little value. The best example of this is when websites stuff their content with popular keywords, to appear on more results pages.

As they have evolved, the Google algorithms have learned to distinguish between valuable keyword rich pages and keyword stuffed content [12]. It seems remarkable that software can do this, but the proof is in the search rankings.

The position given to content is a direct judgment of its value. If a business ranks poorly, it needs to make improvements [13]. It is hard to cheat the system and rarely worth the trouble.

White hat (legitimate) onpage SEO is simple and efficient. It does change all the time, so businesses are advised to keep an eye on current trends and developments. Many hire a dedicated team to handle their onpage search engine optimization, but it is not the only option. On the other hand, the larger the business, the more time and resources are needed [14].

Why Are Relevance and Authenticity Important?

For Google, the two pillars of value are relevance and authenticity [15]. The importance of relevance has been discussed in some detail already.

It refers to how closely the content matches the searched for keyword. For instance, the keyword 'baby cradle' is unlikely to be relevant to the death metal band Cradle of Filth, even though their website contains the word many times over.

Authenticity is a measure of how genuine and trusted the content appears to be [16]. The best way to increase authenticity is to place links to a target website on other external platforms which also have a high degree of relevance and trust.

In other words, trustworthy websites recommending other websites is something that Google likes to see. The assumption is that nobody would voluntarily endorse content if they do not believe in its value [17].

In fact, linking to an external site is a way to encourage visitors to leave and spend time elsewhere, so it is a vote of confidence.

Google will reward web hosts who are willing to make such endorsements because it helps their algorithms judge content. Consequently, a small amount of 'authority' is passed on to a website every time that it gets a new endorsement [18]. Both parties benefit from this small act of collaboration.

The links must be relevant, however. It is not possible to cheat the system by linking up with an external provider and continually hosting links for one another, particularly if the two platforms are only barely related [19].

If a Tupperware manufacturer has twenty links driving traffic from a handbag retailer, for example, the impact is likely to be minimal. There is no clear connection between the two.

SEO is all about precision. Quality always wins over quantity.

Now, it is time to focus on the practical steps involved in onpage SEO. The objectives and goals are clear, but what actions are taken to achieve them? As mentioned, there are many different techniques. They can be applied individually, in complementary clusters, or as part of a comprehensive SEO checklist. The best approach is to look at every piece of content with a fresh eye.

Most have room for a little bit of each technique (keyword placement, inner linking, outer linking, images, etc.), but they have to be inserted naturally.

If there is no room for a picture or a specific keyword usage sounds odd, don't use it.

Focus on creating engaging, fluid content and applying onpage SEO in a way which enhances the user experience. Make intelligent choices and remember that, just because the aim is to please a computer, content should not sound computerized [20].

Google indexes content that utilize these techniques before searching for other features.

It is helpful for businesses to imagine each new piece of content as the blueprint for a virtual house. The bare bones are there. The potential for a significant result is there, but it has to be constructed in the right way.

Onpage SEO provides bricks and mortar. With every new brick added, the strength and size of the house increases until it is so big that it comes to dominate its virtual neighborhood.

At this point, it is impossible for internet users to miss, so traffic climbs and more visitors stick around to check out its interior.

The longer they browse, the more chances of them initiating an action that will create a profit for the owner.

It is a basic analogy, but one which makes it easier to conceptualize the importance of SEO.

Approaching search engine marketing in a straightforward manner can be tricky sometimes because technical jargon often obscures its simplicity.

It can dissuade first-time bloggers and smaller internet businesses from making a push for the top of results pages.

Yet, all of the terminologies can be broken down into basic steps and actions.

They are accessible to every kind of content creator; from travel writers to fashion designers, graphic artists, personal shoppers, doggy day care centers, and musicians.

Everybody wants to become noticed online.

With onpage SEO, it stops being a possibility and becomes an inevitability.

For e-commerce businesses, increased traffic leads to more conversions and sales.

Rather than being a 'take it or leave it' chore, search engine optimization is a tool kit for surviving online and beating the competition.

Creating Catchy, Engaging Title Tags

It makes sense to start with the first part of the online content that internet users see when they complete a search. The title is hugely influential because it is the most visually striking element [21]. Even though Google search results also include a snippet of text, to help users decide if entries are relevant, many don't look at this. They skim read the title and make their decision based on what it tells them [22].

It means that, even if a title is only five or six words in length, it is worth making sure that they are the right ones.

Every word should be valuable. There should be no filler words and no casually added terms because this is the real estate of the online world.

The three attributes to aim for are relevancy, engagement, and specificity.

Titles with good SEO are short but catchy, and they convey a lot of information in a short space of time.

The balance between SEO and engagement is crucial here.

It is possible to rank highly on search results pages, because a title covers all of the boxes, and still receives a slow rate of traffic [23]. Eventually, this situation leads to a natural decline in SEO ranking, because whether or not the content is titled well doesn't change the fact that nobody is clicking on it.

There are four practical techniques for improving content titles in a way which pleases Google.

The first is making sure that the title is clear and concise.

Internet users move fast online. They rarely stop to read descriptions or tags in their entirety. Instead, they scan left to right and pick up the keywords. Titles with good onpage SEO are readable in a matter of seconds [24].

The title length and the arrangement of words (particularly key search terms) are similarly important. One clever way is to insert a number because this instantly differentiates a blog or article from the many other articles on the same topic [25]. For example, '10 Great Ways to Upgrade Your Bathroom' is more specific and compelling than 'How to Upgrade Your Bathroom.'

Finally, if possible, a brand name should appear as well.

Step One: Make It Clear and Concise

Many content developers completely disregard the rules surrounding title length.

It is a big mistake, because they exist for a reason.

There is a limited amount of physical and visible space available on a screen and, therefore, on a search engine results page. Technically, a title can be as long as a developer wants, but it gets truncated (cut off) after a certain limit [26].

Sometimes, this is not a big deal. If all of the essential information is included, a truncated end might not have a significant impact.

However, it does look strange and unnatural on the page; clumsy, somehow. Avoid it where possible. Stick to the 70-character limit that Google imposes on all online titles [27].

For mobile friendly, responsive content (which should be the aim for everybody), the title could behave a little differently. There is still a truncation limit, but depending on the screen size, the title may have an earlier or later cut off point [28].

The only way to know for sure is to test title ideas out on different screens. Responsiveness is a tremendous asset and titles must be clear and concise on laptops, tablets, and smartphones [29].

Step Two: Position the Keyword Correctly

This is one of the most important rules of all.

The title must include the primary (top priority) keyword.

For instance, if the article or blog post belongs to a pizzeria in New York, a catchy title might be something like 'Grab a Pizza: 7 Great Places to Get a Slice in Manhattan.'

It is witty, engaging, and is full of information. The closer the primary keyword is to the front of the title, the better the search ranking [30].

However, this is not always possible without making the words sound awkward, so don't force it. It should flow and be easy to read.

Specific details are highly recommended, particularly location-based terms and descriptors. The example, '10 Great Ways to Upgrade Your Bathroom' is more valuable than 'How to Upgrade Your Bathroom,' because it is specific about what the user should expect.

'10 Great Ways to Upgrade Your Bathroom on a Budget' is even better, for the same reason. It gives more detailed information and helps Google take the content to the right audience.

Don't forget that search engines are focused on one thing; providing the best quality results. The more that a business can do to classify and describe its content, the more easily Google will give out rewards and increase page rank [31].

These longer, more descriptive phrases are what is known as 'long tailed keywords' [32]. They hold value and location-based algorithms are currently undergoing a real transformation, thanks to lengthier descriptors and specific search terms.

For businesses wanting to drive traffic to the website and the physical location, add on phrases meaning near, local, and close to me because they have enormous potential for physical locations [33].

Step Three: Incorporate the Brand Name

For a while, it was fashionable for content creators to omit the company or brand name from titles.

The truth is that it does not need to be incorporated. Leaving it out isn't going to push a web page or article down the search rankings and into obscurity.

On the other hand, it is a straightforward and easy way to add a little bit more of a push. It adds information, so Google considers it to be more valuable [34].

Plus, it means that the brand name is displayed in large letters, on a results page, as part of the content. It can never hurt to remind internet users (and potential visitors) of this critical detail.

Even if a person does not click through or choose the company first time, they might be convinced to do so when they search again, and they recognize that the same name appears as an authority website.

It is not all about words, though; it is about providing a high quality, consistent user experience. It knows that internet users are turned off by sprawling, uninspiring blocks of text. They are hard to read, even if the content is engaging because the design on a digital screen is different from the design of a book.

Content needs to be snappy, fast and cleverly arranged so that the eyes stay stimulated and focused. Nevertheless, it is harder than it sounds to keep visitors engaged because articles that are too brief lead to high bounce rates [35].

Once again, it is all about finding the right balance. Most commercial articles are no longer than 800 words because this is enough length in which to pack a piece full of information, but it does not take longer than 10-15 minutes to read.

It is entirely possible to get away with longer pieces, but they require a greater degree of visual creativity. Avoid big, blocky chunks of texts at all times. Break them up with compelling images and smart graphic design [36].

Bullet points and headings are a must for content any longer than 400 words because visitors are turned off by visually dense arrangements [37]. If they scan the article and it looks like a chore, they may bounce from the site (click through and leave within seconds).

Infographics are one of the best ways to present large amounts of data. They combine information in a graphic design template, alongside bold colors and an arrangement that is easy on the eyes [38].

Tip One: Use Legal Images

Companies that are new to e-commerce quickly learn that certain rules dictate which images are and are not permitted.

It is illegal to post a copyrighted image or design on a website without acquiring approval first [39]. While the chances of anybody actually noticing this kind of unauthorized use is relatively small, the consequences are not.

It is not worth the trouble of being penalized for such a fundamental mistake. Fortunately, there are plenty of creative commons collections out there on the internet.

These are platforms (like Flickr and FreeImages) which contain thousands of non-copyrighted images [40]. Most can be used without any approval. Others require a small link to the owner's website or gallery.

Tip Two: Create the Images

More than anything, Google loves it when businesses create original content [41]. It understands that the resources are not always in place for this, so companies are not punished too harshly for using recycled images.

However, adding pictures that can't be found anywhere else on the internet is a great way to get a boost in the search rankings.

Place original images under copyright, and they cannot be used by anybody else [42]. It increases their value in terms of search engine quality.

Keep in mind that JPEG, GIF, and PNG file formats are the best options because they load fast.

JPEGs are, by far, the most common image type found on the internet, but they do suffer a little with lossy data compression. On the other hand, they are small and widely supported [43].

Tip Three: Change the File Names

It might seem like a tiny detail, but content developers are strongly advised to edit image filenames. It is of particular importance when posting original pictures taken with digital devices. Often, the automatic file name is made up of numbers, and they mean little to a search engine [44].

For instance, a photo taken at a music festival might be tagged with something as generic as 'IMG_58742_8663.'

It is not useful for Google because it tells the algorithm nothing about the picture or what it contains.

Consequently, it is likely to ignore it altogether or even judge it negatively when deciding on page ranking.

The change does not have to be huge. Something like 'IMG_Chicago_MusicFestival_2016_04' provides enough information. There will be internet users out there who are searching for this particular content. Get it to them quickly, and they are much more likely to remember the source and come back for a second, longer visit.

Tip Four: Separate Thumbnails

Load time contributes substantially to SEO and large thumbnails can slow down a website.

Ideally, they should be as small as feasibly possible. It is easy to resize thumbnail pictures with a photo editing tool like PhotoShop or Pixlr [45].

It is not worth worrying too much about quality here because thumbnails are not supposed to be the main reference point.

They are designed to be small and, if users want to see more, they can click through and browse for larger images.

One clever way to maintain fast loading speeds and provide clear, high-quality pictures is to make them available in a separate window. It is a common trick and can be seen all over the internet.

The images on the article or blog are quite small, but hovering over them with a mouse (or clicking) brings up a bigger version that doesn't affect the content [46].

The rule of thumb for e-commerce websites is a maximum file size of 70kb [47]. It will not always be easy to stick to this guideline, but it offers an easy way to post multiple, high-resolution pictures in one space.

Ultimately, the only way to know for sure if a visual layout works is to test it [48]. Put together a prototype of the preferred arrangement and see how it looks on a multitude of screen sizes.

Keyword placement is the lifeblood of onpage SEO techniques. This element of search engine optimization has spawned entire books and help manuals [49]. It is an industry all of its own, so the key to success is to identify the most relevant and applicable rules to the target content.

Google takes keywords very seriously, and large parts of its algorithm updates are dedicated to increasingly sophisticated ways of reviewing them [50].

It means that, of all the onpage SEO techniques, this is the one that deserves the most time and attention. Like all the rest, the more it is done the easier it gets, but keyword research is always a valuable process.

Authority (how valued the content is) does count, but it is relevance which rules at Google [51]. It is important to keep coming back to the primary objective – the algorithms are trying to produce the closest match possible to the given word or phrase.

If businesses had no way of finding out what words users are searching for, their online marketing would be much more inconsistent.

However, they can use certain tools and methods to identify the most popular search terms and make sure that they are included [52]. Think of all the online stores in the world selling camping tents. It is reasonable to assume that every single one has a website which features the words 'camping tents' very heavily.

It is still a valuable feature because it distinguishes the companies selling camping tents from the millions of others selling completely different products.

The keyword placement needs to go further, though, as hundreds of thousands of relevant results still get returned. The content developer should look carefully at the products, at the defining features of the company, and at the location [53].

There are thousands of possible keyword combinations. 'Camping tents for families.' 'Five person camping tents.' 'Three person camping tents with porch.' 'Waterproof camping tents.' 'Compact camping tents.' Etc.

When the location is added to the mix, the degree of specificity grows, and it becomes even easier to rank higher because there are fewer results to compete with for attention [54].

For example, 'Buy family camping tents in Louisville' is more valuable than just 'camping tents.' It identifies a user and a location, both of which Google will target and index when matching the content to searches. It is not to say that shorter, more direct keywords are not helpful.

They are essential too, but smart SEO covers short and long tailed search terms. People do not speak or complete searches in an exclusive manner. Sometimes they take a broad approach and, at other times, they are much more accurate.

The Big Problem with Early Keyword Research

As mentioned, Google dedicates a lot of time reviewing and updating its keyword indexing systems. There are several reasons for this.

The first is that keywords account for a significant proportion of the searching process. Working out how users are searching and what for is an essential part of streamlining the technology [55]. On top of this, Google knows that it is, technically, the weakest element of its algorithms.

It is extremely hard for computer software to mimic speech patterns [56]. Human beings do not formulate sentences based entirely on grammatical rules. They make decisions based on situation and context.

In other words, they rarely input searches for content in the same way that they would ask a friend or another person. Most omit words, spell incorrectly (in some cases), and select whatever phrasing is most convenient [57].

It is because they know that they are talking to a computer and certain rules have no value. Spell a word wrong or leave out the word 'the' from a search and a computer will not mind. In short, people are unpredictable.

While this casual speech does obey some rules, they are harder for a search engine to understand, because they require a grasp of context.

It means that, rather dichotomously, keyword research is both the strongest (most valuable) and weakest part of the Google algorithms [58].

The focus on algorithm updates is always on learning how to imitate natural speech better so that searches produce the best possible results.

For SEO specialists and content developers, the aim should be to keep up with these evolutions and understand why they are important.

Crucially, the value of natural sounding keywords only really matters for e-commerce, because Google says that it does [59]. If they change the rules, the rules change for everybody.

Before this emphasis on natural speech patterns, however, keyword SEO was much simpler.

Google searches functioned on a one to one basis, by dividing a query into its base elements and working out where they appeared most often on the internet [60]. The winning formula, then, was frequency. The more a developer could insert a popular keyword into content, the more times Google would spot it and rank it as relevant.

It is still the case, but to a lesser degree, because Google quickly realized that there is a significant difference between keyword placement and keyword stuffing.

Unfortunately, with the old algorithm, there was no need to imitate natural speech or even form logical content. It was technically possible to rank highly with a website page which didn't make much sense but did contain the target keyword over and over [61].

It was good for business but bad for Google.

It lowered the quality of searches because users got left with irrelevant and unhelpful results. Titling a website page 'Pizza Restaurant Denver' does help the algorithm find a match for the content, but the user still has to be happy with it.

The chance of rejection is high, as it sounds clunky and unnatural. Regardless of whether they search in such a casual manner, users demand well-constructed, high-quality content. It must be engaging, make contextual sense, and, above all else, offer value.

The All New and Improved Algorithms

Now, to continue to rank highly, it is a matter of understanding what Google has done to remedy the problem. The biggest change is that authenticity is combined with relevancy when reviewing keyword placement [62]. It is no longer possible to keyword stuff and get a great result unless the content makes sense contextually and grammatically.

Even then, the keyword density has to be just right, as overuse makes content boring to read.

From a technical perspective, the new and improved algorithms incorporate 'semantic search.' It occurs in two stages.

First, Google identifies the core components of the search, as it always did. In the case of 'pizza restaurant, Denver,' it works out that the user is looking for an 'eat in' establishment which sells pizza and is located in Denver.

However, it selects the most relevant and valuable results based on their level of authenticity (how content is constructed, whether other people have endorsed it, etc.) [63]

In truth, the authenticity part of the process gets influenced by hundreds of different pieces of information, but the result is always to determine which one is the 'best,' according to what users value the most.

For a pizza restaurant, customer reviews and comments are going to play a big part [64]. It all comes down to the fact that Google has made it difficult to cheat the system. Keyword placement has to be thoughtful, and it must offer value.

While some businesses are bound to lament this, it makes onpage SEO easier.

The scope is broad, so there are millions more ways to distinguish one piece of content from the hundreds of thousands of similar results.

The secret to success is learning how to carry out good keyword research and how to tailor it to fit a specific industry, company, and website.

The Major Benefits of Effective Keyword Research

There are many different ways to carry out keyword research. As is so often the case with search engine optimization, the route appears complex, but the aim is very simple.

Keyword research helps content creators determine what words and phrases to use as well as where to place them, and how to boost their value. It can take a long time or be relatively basic. It all depends on the needs of the company.

If one thing is clear at this point, it should be that SEO is a vast and limitless world of techniques, methods, and opportunities.

It never stops changing, because the internet is always in a state of flux. The important thing is that success is about selecting the ones that are most applicable and most likely to be valuable. Some businesses invest a lot of time and money into keyword research.

Others prefer to treat it casually and combine technical, analytical data with organic, instinctive knowledge.

Neither approach is wrong. Keyword research provides several benefits, including a better understanding of the market, a better understanding of competitors, and the chance to construct higher quality content.

In the simplest terms, working out what words users are looking for all the time is the best way to get popular ones into commercial articles, blogs, and web pages [65].

If 'watching how to bake a cake' is appearing more frequently than 'learning how to bake a cake,' it is the former which is the target.

This example would also say something important about the market. Preference for the word 'watch' implies a demand for video content.

The team in charge of SEO could take advantage and start posting more video content, tutorials, and funny clips.

One overlooked benefit of keyword research is competition analysis.

Many businesses assume that the most popular words and phrases are always the best choices. They are not really incorrect, but it is worth acknowledging that every other enterprise will be thinking the same thing [66].

The most popular keywords, as defined by Google data, are targeted by everybody, including market rivals, because they are the hot property – the ones to watch.

By all means, use them, but be smart as well. Keyword research is one way to determine which keywords and phrases rival companies are already ranking for at a high level.

Usually, they are the shortest, most basic ones. Brief one and two-word search terms are much easier to slot into content than long tailed keywords. It means that companies which can find a way to utilize the most popular longer keywords, in a natural and organic fashion, have the edge over all of the others [67].

Content developers can stop worrying about how to wrestle with a million other businesses for those top three phrases and take a step back [68]. As long as the selections are popular and rank well, the fact that there might not be so many rivals bidding for them does not matter. Finally, keyword research supports the construction of higher quality content.

Make it part of an integrated onpage SEO checklist, and it becomes inexorably linked with content creation.

When there is a clear, valuable set of keywords and terms to choose from, it is easier to frame and shape web pages, blogs, articles, and other resources. The basic building blocks are there. It is not a matter of writing the article first and sticking the keywords in afterward. The content is raised around the SEO until the two are inseparable entities [69].

In many ways, this represents the most successful use of search engine optimization. The more natural and integrated it is, the more Google will reward it.

It prevents the awkward, stubborn inconsistencies that occur precisely because the nature of the process is awkward. Search engine optimization is merely human beings trying to please an algorithm, which is itself designed to please humans, by imitating their habits.

Careful Placement and Density

While some experts claim that there's a golden rule for keyword density, there is no evidence to suggest that Google has a hard and fast limit [70].

It is up to the content creator to decide how many placements are appropriate. Ultimately, if a guiding principle is used, and a piece of content does not adhere to it, but it still sounds natural and engaging, it is likely fine to use it.

One of the quickest ways to get an SEO boost is to place the target (most important) keyword within the first line, or at least the first 100-200 words [71].

This has to be the most commonly used technique because it takes just seconds to perform. Given its simplicity, it should be used in every piece of SEO crafted content. The reason it works is simple too. Placing the keyword in the first paragraph tells Google what it is about and how to categorize it [72].

When writing, don't forget that the aim is to place keywords in a way that feels and sounds natural.

Many online marketers fail to understand is that flow and cohesion are far more important than any guiding rules or ratios.

There are no penalties for having more or less than the recommended amount of keywords, but Google can spot poor placement very quickly.

The best way to determine whether a piece of content flows naturally is to read it out loud [73].

There is a clever trick, which many companies use to boost their reach and presence on results pages. When it comes to company websites, more content is better, as long as it is carefully crafted.

Therefore, splitting core information about the business into its separate services or products is one way to increase exposure [74]. Google likes this because it optimizes content and presents the algorithms with neat, categorized pages to index.

For instance, a residential cleaning company is likely to offer a number of different services, even if they all come under the generalized banner of 'cleaning.' Therefore, they could split their website content up and create separate pages for 'Carpet Cleaning,' 'Appliance Cleaning,' 'Furniture Cleaning,' 'Whole House Cleaning,' and so on. Title pages are powerful when it comes to determining relevance [75]. The more the website has, the greater its impact.

Once again, the secret to success is never to force techniques to work when it is quite clear that they don't apply.

Some companies will not have enough information to create multiple title pages.

Spreading it even thinner will require repetition and keyword stuffing, both of which are discouraged.

Use instinct and logic when making these decisions, rather than sticking doggedly to technical rules when implementing onpage SEO.

The importance of incorporating a target keyword into the title has been discussed, as have the best ways to position it in the content body.

One keyword is not enough because it does not provide a lot of specificity. The real power lies in what is known as 'long tailed keywords.' These are short phrases, rather than one or two-word searches [76].

They are defined by their precision, so instead of searching for 'bars in New York,' a user might search for 'cheap cocktail bars in Manhattan,' or 'happy hour cocktail bar near me.'

The more specificity is given, the more optimized the results and the easier it is for the user to find a valuable answer to their search.

Content creators can utilize long tailed keywords by getting specific about their own products or services.
Wherever possible, prioritize location-based information, especially if you want to drive foot traffic through the door. The beauty of phrases like 'near me,' 'close to me,' and 'in my town' are that the users who apply them are likely looking to make a purchase quickly, rather than just browsing for a potential opportunity. [77].

Tailoring content in a way which reaches these people is a great marketing strategy. It gets more customers through the door by targeting the ones who are most open to the idea of buying from you, now.

Numbers are a useful addition to content, particularly in the title. You can usually sneak a number in somewhere, no matter what the article or blog is about and it adds another distinction [78].

It is another layer of 'individuality' to differentiate the information from all the rest. For example, '10 Great Ways to Upgrade Your Bathroom' is more impactful than 'How to Upgrade Your Bathroom,' because it is specific about what the user should expect.

In most cases, long tailed keywords are better suited to use in the title (once) and sprinkled throughout the body of the content.

Subheadings should be kept brief. They are designed to break up large pieces of text and provide a visual aid, so they shouldn't be too lengthy.

When used with skill, long-tailed keywords can be very powerful. They don't attract the same fierce competition as 'head' or target keywords. There aren't as many marketers vying for their use [79].

The most effective onpage SEO utilizes both longer and shorter keywords because they have different strengths and advantages.

Target keywords are heavy hitters. They categorize content plainly and simply and ensure that it reaches the right audience. Long-tailed keywords come in afterward and add another layer of detail and refinement [80]. While they produce a lower search volume, this isn't a bad thing if those doing the searching have been targeted correctly.

Some marketers and content developers are still unaware of the importance of 'LSI keywords.' These are just variations – synonyms – of the target words and phrases [81].

If possible, they should be sprinkled liberally throughout articles and other pieces.

They do need to be used in conjunction with careful placement of the standard key terms, however.

LSI keywords aren't independent and won't lead to a ranking boost unless the search algorithm can connect the dots and identify the SEO links within the content.

The easiest way to find valuable LSI keywords is to perform a normal Google search for the targeted keyword or phrase.

On the results page, scroll to the bottom of the entries and look at the 'Searches Related To' section [82]. These are most popular alternative ways of getting to the content.

One example might be if the target keyword is 'sales training.' Popular variations could be anything from 'sales teaching' to 'sales certification' 'how to learn sales' and 'sales courses near me.' They might not be a precise match, but most users would consider the information closely related to their search [83]. There are several free tools which content developers can use to generate LSI keywords. UberSuggest is free and is a great asset for on-page SEO [84].

To construct great onpage SEO, which works every time, stay true to the target audience.

Ultimately, all the free tools and clever tricks in the world cannot make up for a marketer who doesn't care about what their audience wants.

It takes time to get familiar with consumers and identify their needs, but it is an essential responsibility. Keyword research only works, because it puts the user at the heart of the content [85].

Of all the useful SEO techniques, this is one that is worthy of the most commitment.

Carry out market research, take a peek at what competitors are doing, and craft a keyword framework, rather than approaching every new article or page from scratch.

The aim should be to make keyword placement fast and simple, without compromising on quality. It isn't always easy, but it usually worth the effort.

The next SEO strategy is much more straightforward than keyword research and placement. H1 and H2 tags are the names given to two sections of code which make content bolder and more visible [86].

The good news is that you don't have to be a master coder or have any real knowledge of coding to use them. It is important to understand why they work and the benefits they have on a webpage or article.

The best way to describe H1 and H2 tags is the H1 tag is the title and H2 is the subtitle.

Both are used to grab the attention of people passing by, only in the case of online content, the target is search engine users. The problem is that search results pages are standardized. From a visual perspective, everything looks the same [87].

All of the top 'blue link' entries are presented in the same way, in the form of titles and snippets of text [88]. Placing H1 and H2 tags in the right places makes some of this text bigger and more noticeable than the rest.

The obvious place to start is with the title. While there is no obligation to insert tags – Google can usually tell which bit is the title from where it is placed on the page – they are highly recommended.

Without them, there is a bigger risk of Google misinterpreting the arrangement of the page and getting the title wrong [89].

It also takes more time to index and review the content, which could have a negative impact on results ranking.

All that the search algorithms want is to assess the page quickly and give it a score, so helping out with this is a good way to earn extra points.

Some content creators don't use H1 and H2 tags, but it seems like a wasted opportunity considering how simple they are to insert.

The H1 tag is always used to identify the title. Inserting it correctly makes the title the biggest element on search results pages.

The H2 tag works in exactly the same way, except it is inserted around the main subheading. It follows on from the H1 tag in a logical way, by making the subheading bigger, but still slightly smaller than the title [90].

There are multiple layers of tags which can be used after H1 and H2, but it is becoming quite rare to see this in content.

Most articles have a basic structure, which includes a title and several subheadings all of the same size and visibility. Extra tags (H3, H4, and so on) are not usually required, but are recommended [91].

Incorporating this simple SEO tactic will not transform search rankings all on its own, but it is another helpful way to give the content a boost [92].

It contributes to the construction of a neat, logically arranged page; a piece of content that is easy to read and directs visitors through a pleasant, valuable online experience.

When using H1 and H2 tags, think about how they relate to other basic elements like paragraph structure and make sure that the right coding methods are used to maintain an optimized arrangement [93]. If there is one thing Google has no time for, it's a sloppy attitude when it comes to the fundamental structure of the text.

Don't forget that adding a H1 tag will demarcate the title and tell Google 'this is the section of text you need to enlarge.' Before you insert them, make sure that the title isn't too long for the results page [94]. Use the 70-character limit as a guide, because Google usually cuts off text which extends beyond this.

Just to make clear, the H1 tag doesn't count as part of the title text (characters), but it will cut off any letters outside the two tags.

Invest in Responsive Website Design

Ten years ago, it wasn't all that unusual for a business not to have a website. Now, it is very rare indeed, regardless of whether a company actually sells their products online.

Similarly, responsive mobile web design is no longer a tool which businesses can use to get an edge over the competition. It is considered to be an essential part of the browsing experience [95].

It means that businesses not already investing in responsive, adaptable web development needs to get on board fast.

It is easier than it looks and it provides a seamless, cohesive transition between desktop and mobile content. The importance of this cannot be underestimated. The number of web searches made via mobile devices is now greater than that completed searches on computers [96].

What is Responsive Web Design?

When an internet user visits a website, they are now more likely to be accessing the content on a smartphone, tablet, or another portable device.

On a basic level, no special changes are needed to find and load websites in this way. As long as there's an internet connection, the process is always successful. The problem is that viewing a web page designed for a desktop computer on a phone leads to issues with size [97].

The screen is significantly smaller, so anything that does not fit cuts off. If scrolling capabilities are permitted, the navigation is likely to be clunky and awkward, because it is designed for a mouse on a big display. The content may be there, but whether or not the user can really do anything with it is debatable.

At one time, the best solution was to create multiple versions of the same website, each with different dimensions [98].

While this works, it is hugely inefficient. No business wants to invest triple the time and resources just to create copies of the same content.

Fortunately, responsive web design is a much better option. It is a collection of techniques and coding processes which are used to construct a single shifting, changing website [99].

One way to think of it is as a shop mannequin or design dummy for web pages.

The underlying structure stays the same, but the aesthetic can be changed by 'hanging' a different product over the top. No matter how many different 'looks' are applied, it is always possible to return to that baseline frame and pick a new one.

This is the essence of responsive design, and it means that one website can be built to cater to many needs. For a user, each transition should be so efficient that they barely notice the mannequin changing at all.

Why Is Responsive Design Important?

There is a very simple answer for why businesses need responsive websites – the consumer demands it.

Internet users prioritize adaptable content that they can view just as easily on an iPhone as they can on a laptop. Where the people go, Google follows. It rewards content developers for seamless, multidimensional web design and fervently pushes them up the search rankings [100].

The aim of responsive design is to make browsing content an equally enjoyable experience no matter how it is accessed.

This means intuitive, smooth scrolling functions. It means a focus on transitional screen sizes. Good web design has a 'snap back' effect, which enables pages to snap to fit any size display [101]. Loading speeds are important too. Modern smartphones are very powerful, but they still can't compete with full-size computers.

To ensure that content loads quickly and images and other items are functional, it is necessary to strip some features back.

It is worth pointing out that Google is keen to making website optimization easier. For instance, its recent AMP update rolled out basic mobile design tools to regular content developers. The AMP software creates a streamlined version of web pages, which load in a particular way (content before images, ads, and other heavier features) [102].

For now at least, using AMP does not provide any direct boost to rankings. However, when mobile users complete searches, Google does automatically provide AMP pages over standard ones, if they are available.

The likelihood is that it will eventually start to show a preference for these optimized pages, particularly if visitors vote with their fingers and AMP content gets faster click through rates [103]. Though, the software is still in its early stages.

There are three key principles underpinning responsive web design. They are fluid images, fluid grids, and media queries. It's time to take a look at each one in more detail.

Fluid Grids [104]

In the past, websites were defined by their number of pixels. However, this isn't a useful way to think about digital content anymore.

It is, in many ways, a leftover from our reliance on print media and it doesn't represent the capacity for change.

Rather than being restricted to an amount of a fixed unit, contemporary web pages are built with relative units (much like percentages).

The following formula can help content developers start building in percentages, as opposed to single units.

Target / Context = Result

Imagine, for instance, a website with a wrapper which limits its width to 960 pixels.

The website is being viewed on a browser window with a screen that has a width of 1920 pixels.

Here, the wrapper is known as the 'target,' and the browser is the 'context.'

The percentage value is the relative amount of pixels required for the two to be compatible and the website to look and function as intended.

It is calculated with the following formula:

$$960 \text{ pixels} / 1920 \text{ pixels} = 50\%$$

Even better, is the fact that the same rules apply to child components inside the wrapper.

For example, imagine a two column arrangement positioned inside the 960-pixel limit.

The right column is a large area designed for the main body of content. It is 640 pixels in width.

The left component is a sidebar. It is 300 pixels in width.

There needs to be 20 pixels of empty space left between the two components.

Right Component: 640 pixels / 960 pixels = 66.66667%

Left Component: 300 pixels / 960 pixels = 31.25%

Empty Space: 20 pixels / 960 pixels = 2.08334%

The percentage values can be incorporated into CSS tweaks as part of the padding, margin, and width information.

With relative percentages, it becomes easy to construct that metaphorical mannequin.

The frame remains the same, but the configuration laid over the top is fluid and adaptable.

Fluid Images [105]

Fluid images are similar to transitional grids, and the two rely on one another to function.

The key idea here is that responsive images are 'elastic.' They can expand or shrink to fit the confines of that shifting, changing grid.

Only a single line of CSS code is needed to achieve it.

img { max-width: 100% }.

The code instructs the browser not to make any of the images bigger than their pixel value.

Thus, pictures won't ever get stretched, blurred, or pulled out of shape, no matter what the size of the screen used to view them.

Crucially, however, it still leaves room for fast shrinking when the parent wrapper is smaller than the pixel value of the image.

In other words, if a 900-pixel picture is positioned inside a wrapper with a limit of 700 pixels, the picture reduces to meet the size of the containing component.

The other dimensions are determined according to the pixel value and what specific actual height and width are needed to present a high-quality image.

If the coding is correct, this calculation is done automatically.

Even with all of these tricks, it can still be tricky to convince mobile phones to display web pages as intended.

They have a particular aversion to pages which contain multiple columns because mobiles are designed for frequent vertical scrolling, in order to account for the small screen size [106]. Wide layouts present a challenge. However, media queries are a clever solution.

The term media query refers to a type of CSS technology that has been widely used for some time. It enables certain components of CSS to be activated only under specific conditions [107].

For instance, a content developer could use a media query to trigger CSS components when a browser moves beyond a predefined width.

In the case of wide layouts then, media queries identify areas in which the site width is problematic and apply the relevant CSS codes when a change to the content is required. Imagine starting with a two column arrangement (as mentioned).

The aim is to make sure that the sidebar appears at the top of the page when the content is accessed via mobile. It is necessary if all of the content is going to fit and function seamlessly.

It is important to understand that only so much optimization is possible.

Try to cram too much on the screen or force unsuitable layouts and things will start to look dysfunctional. It is what is known as the 'breakpoint;' the limit after which space becomes poorly utilized [108].

The Rise of the 'Mobile First' Generation

The relationship between search engine optimization and responsive web design is very clear.

Consumers are moving towards a place of constant mobile access. They are already showing a natural preference for optimized, responsive content. Therefore, search engines consider it more valuable.

It has become common for website developers to start with the mobile experience and work upwards to desktop layouts and designs [109].

It makes sense, as all the signs suggest that desktops will eventually become obsolete.

Choosing to invest in intelligent mobile design is the only viable option for modern businesses wanting to stay ahead of the curve. To ensure future success, become a reliable brand which places no limits on how users interact with content.

Guarantee a Fast, Efficient Experience

As the importance of responsive design shows, high-quality onpage SEO encompasses more than just the content itself.

In fact, all of the elements and components surrounding the content have an impact on its value and must be perfectly selected and structured.

One of the factors which greatly contributes to overall user experience is efficiency – how fast does the website load and is it quick enough?

Internet users are demanding, but they are also complicated.

They bounce from site to site with no consequence, so abandoning a piece of content is easy if it doesn't fit their criteria.

On the other hand, the longer you can convince a visitor to stay on the website, the more they are investing in terms of their own time and interest. As the level of personal investment increases, the likelihood of a bounce (fast exit) gets smaller [110].

Therefore, the goal for a content developer should be to make the quality of the user experience clear right from the outset.

Website loading speeds are a big part of this. If the page doesn't load fast, that could be it for a company in terms of getting them to interact with the content. When the bounce rate is high because visitors are landing and leaving again within seconds, Google notices [111].

It has a negative impact on the search ranking, as too much bounce suggests that users aren't finding the content to be very valuable.

The good news is that, like all ranking weaknesses, bounce rate can be fixed by improving loading speeds. If sluggish web pages are thought to be the culprit, the best first step is to find a free performance evaluator. Many tools online perform a simple check on loading efficiency [112].

Completing a basic check is recommended, as slow loading speeds are just one possible cause of a high bounce rate. The solutions range from simple tweaks like compressing large images or displaying them in a pop-up window to bigger changes like finding a better host.

6 Methods for Improving Slow Loading Speeds

1. Reduce the Number of HTTP Requests

Around 80% of the loading time for a typical web page is spent handling its various piece parts [113]. This includes the pictures, stylesheets, scripts, and any flash elements.

Loading each of them requires a separate HTTP request. Therefore, the more elements are included on the page, the longer it will take to load. On the other hand, that is not to say that having a lot of elements is always a bad thing.

The reality is that sophisticated and complex platforms do contain a lot of details.

It is up to the content developer and the site manager to decide where that compromise lies. It is always necessary to sacrifice some degree of speed for higher quality, but the balance must be made carefully. If the web pages load too slowly and users lose interest, this will show in the search rankings [114].

This is all to say that reducing the number of HTTP requests is the simplest and easiest way to get a boost of speed [115].

However, it does mean taking elements away. The best advice is to make sure that every component has a purpose.

Don't insert images purely to make up empty space. Consider whether multiple stylesheets can be assimilated into just one. Also, reduce scripts and place them at the bottom of web pages [116].

2. Compress Large Pages

Rich, high-quality content tends to tip the scales when it comes to data volume.

Large pages (over 100KB) are filled with valuable elements, but they take a long time to load. They are bulky, and they can stifle the good work of onpage SEO elsewhere. One solution is to zip bulky pages using a technique called compression [117].

It shrinks the bandwidth of the page, which cuts its HTTP response time.

A good tool to use for compressing images is Gzip because around 90% of internet traffic is compatible with the software.

What it does is shrink web pages into the Gzip format, so that they are sent for download in a much smaller size. It is a simple strategy, and it can reduce loading times by as much as 70% [118].

3. Activate Browser Caching

Browser caching is a smart way to speed up loading times for repeat visitors.

It isn't a cure-all because first-time users still need to land on a really fast website.

Nevertheless, if the number of repeat visitors is increasing, it means that the content is performing well. Keep it up, and Google will attach more value to the website.

When users first land on a new web page, their hard drive makes a copy of the basic elements. This includes the style sheets, JavaScript files, images, HTML documents, and other components [119]. The page won't load fully until this process is complete. For around thirty elements, this might take approximately 3.2 seconds.

The copied data is stored (or cached) and doesn't need to be loaded on the second, third, or fourth visit to the website.

Theoretically, the subsequent visits should see the page load around two or three seconds faster. This is why websites should always allow caching. It is an insurance policy of sorts, a way to keep users satisfied if they do come back.

The maximum that a website can cache data for is one year, but this is quite unusual. Most only cache for a week at a time, then the information is deleted [120].

It keeps the content fresh because users who haven't made a second visit within a week grow increasingly less likely to do so and losing their cached data is a reasonable risk.

4. Minify the Website Code

The term 'wiz-ee-wig' is an affectionate moniker used to describe web site development programs which support a 'see as you build' process [121].

WordPress is a good example of a WYSIWYG, as it allows users to design and create in a visual form, while the code reacts to changes and alterations. It is a highly valuable system, particularly for content developers with very basic coding skills.

The problem is that it gets messy. When visual elements are constantly being chopped and changed, bits of code get left behind, moved around, and rendered dysfunctional. It isn't a neat way of doing things, and all these little errors can contribute to slower loading speeds [122]. To rectify them, somebody with the right knowledge of coding needs to review the HTML, CSS, and JavaScript and eliminate 'dead' sections.

It is always best if a real person, with genuine reactions, can complete this task, but there are some tools out there to help the inexperienced.

Google recommends use of the PageSpeed Insights extension for Chrome. It identifies weak sections of code and streamlines the HTML for a faster website. Similarly, the Closure Compiler and YUI Compressor programs handle messy javascript and CSS [123].

5. Refine the Larger Images

Images can be a real frustration for content developers. Yet, they are important.

It just isn't feasible for content to be hosted without pictures sometimes, even though they put the biggest drain on loading resources.

The larger the images, the longer it takes, so one simple solution is to be selective when choosing.

Adding original high-quality photographs, for example, is good for SEO on the one hand, because it showcases entirely unique content, but it does put a strain on the response times.

Focus on three elements when refining website images. They are size, format, and coding. Ultimately, pictures need kept as small as possible. Crop them to match the dimensions of the page [124].

If a page that is 600 pixels in width, resize the image to match. Don't just automatically upload a picture which is massively overinflated (2000 pixels) and a poor match for the content.

Always set the width parameter to the width of the page and ensure that all images are relevant, clear, and load correctly every time. There should be no comments or extraneous information attached to them [125].

JPEG is, to some degree, the superior choice for hosting images. PNG is suitable and will work in most cases, but older browsers don't recognize it.

Nevertheless, it isn't such a big risk to use PNG, because it is these users who will have to update eventually, not the other way around. GIFS are handy, as they are very small. However, they don't carry much quality and should be limited to basic, simple graphics (below ten pixels) [126].

Finally, don't forget to touch up the coding after the image is inserted. Empty src codes are common, but they create an unnecessary mess and increase loading speeds.

When the source information is empty (there is nothing between the quotation marks), the browser sends a request to the directory of the page. It adds pointless traffic to the servers, and it can even lead to problems with corrupt data [127].

Keep an eye on the state of codes and check back to ensure that vital information isn't missing. All images need an active URL source – test that the external website works before making a link.

6. Make Redirects Smoother

Every new redirect produces an HTTP request and increases website loading times.

This is a bigger problem for pages with a responsive design, as redirects are used to guide visitors through the main website to the mobile friendly one.

They are important, but they need to work fast. Sluggish redirects are bad for ranking high in the search results.

One fast, prompt redirect is recommended, soon after a mobile user lands on the site. The aim should be to get them to the responsive platform swiftly, and it is best to make the jump right away. Avoid all intermediate and unnecessary redirects, particularly once they have started to browse and interact with content [128].

Crucially, if the following piece of code is incorporated into desktop pages, Google can pick out the mobile-friendly content. It is a good way to boost onpage SEO, as it tells the search engine how to interpret the pages [129]. When Google does not have to work things out independently, it can index websites much faster, and this is great for ranking results.

Know the Value of Backlinks and Internal Links

After keyword research, backlinking is the most time-consuming aspect of SEO. Unlike most other techniques, it requires care and a significant amount of patience, so it should be used as the backbone of SEO campaigns. Together with keywords, backlinks are the framework and the structure of high-quality content [130].

The subject of link building is predictably complex. There are lots of different ways to do it, as well as some which are not advised. It is a little different to other techniques because it doesn't exist in isolation. In fact, the content creator has to rely on help from other people in this case. Successful link building (and backlinking) is only possible if valuable, relevant connections are made to external sources.

There are two types of links; inbound and outbound. Both hold value for SEO, in their own ways, but inbound links are the gold standard. They are the ones that push websites up the search pages and convince Google that the content is unmissable [131]. The difference between the two is simple. While inbound links direct users towards the website, from other outside sources, outbound links do the opposite. They take users off the website and elsewhere [132].

Now, it might sound counterproductive to be directing visitors off the target website and over to one which belongs to somebody else, but many SEO experts argue that the practice has benefits. Nevertheless, it has been a controversial view at times, with other marketing pros arguing that it takes focus away from the content and doesn't give value back [133].

Inbound links come from outside the website. They have to be freely and willingly hosted by another independent platform [134].

The best example is if a blogger writes a review of a product.

Naturally, visitors would expect to find a link to the product website somewhere on the page, especially if the review is favorable. More often than not, the reviewer has made a special arrangement to write the review and host the link because it benefits the parent company [135].

Inbound links are a vote of confidence.

They are a clear endorsement of the value of a website. Google makes the assumption that nobody would happily direct their own users to poor content. Therefore, the more people link to it, the better it must be [136]. This is key to understanding why links are important and what they do for search rankings. Solid, relevant backlinks are a sign of trust and authority, two things which Google highly prizes.

It isn't easily fooled, though, and sometimes businesses try to boost their ranking by randomly scattering links here, there, and everywhere and might not see the benefits they expected.

More than anything else, inbound links must be relevant. It degrades the value of both platforms if they are not closely related in terms of theme, subject matter, and demographic [137]. For instance, links to a cosmetic website from a cooking blog are unlikely to turn into big SEO rewards.

Unless a clear link (and a purpose) for connecting the two has been established in the content, users are going to be directed from one to the other and not really understand why.

Most will show their confusion or displeasure by simply leaving both websites and not returning. Internal links have to show value, in order to produce value. The other part of the process is that it relies on smooth interactions.

There is less certainty when it comes to inbound links. They depend upon the actions of an independent source. It certainly isn't impossible to convince another content provider to backlink for free, but most are shrewd. They want something in return for endorsing the content. In the vast majority of cases, 'payment' is made in the form of exchange. If they are willing to post a backlink on their page, a reciprocal link is an easy way to match their support [138].

This does touch upon those issues surrounding outbound links again, which will be discussed in more detail later. From this perspective, however, it is clear that outbound links do have a purpose if they earn a web site the right to a reciprocal backlink from an authority source. One other method which is quite common is to offer bloggers a free product or trial, in exchange for their public endorsement (and link to) the parent website.

The Three Types of Inbound Links

There are three main types of inbound links [139]. All have value, but they work in slightly different ways, and some are worth more than others because Google has a greater preference for them.

The most favored and valuable of all is the so-called 'natural' link. This is a completely organic endorsement which has been created with no interference or influence from the content developer or site host [140].

In other words, an unaffiliated source has decided that they like the content enough to share it with their own audience. They have done so with no expectation of reciprocation or reward. Google loves natural backlinks, and they are a huge boost to SEO.

They are the ideal; a perfect representation of how online endorsements 'should' function. Of course, they don't always work like this, because human beings are shrewd and clever.

Incentive is at the heart of most backlinking campaigns. The authority sources (popular bloggers, article writers, and online influencers) don't give endorsements away for free.

They want a reciprocal pat on the back, which is why natural links are rarer and harder to achieve. If they do occur, it says very positive things about how the website is viewed by users.

Keep up the good work, and a significant climb up the search rankings is likely to follow.

This reciprocal arrangement (an exchange of value) is common, and it is known as manual outreach [141]. It can be carried out in a number of different ways. Some websites search for relevant bloggers whom they can contact and ask for support. Others submit content to search directories. In some cases, the content creator straight up pays for an agreed upon number of backlinks [142].

The third and final type of backlink is the self-generated or 'non-editorial' link. It holds the lowest value and, while worth having, it shouldn't form the basis of a successful backlinking campaign for SEO. These links come from places like blog comment sections, user profiles, forum signatures, and other add-on elements [143]. As they are not in the main body of text, they are given less weight. For instance, it doesn't take much to post a link to a website within a comment on another blog, but it only attracts a few clicks.

Over the last few years, Google has really fallen out of love with non-editorial backlinks, and they should be treated with care.

Placing too many is a fast track to a swift kick back down the search rankings for posting 'spammy' content [144]. On the other hand, one link posted in the right place can have a surprising result, so do not be afraid of this technique. Just try to be cautious and limit its use. Focus on the other two linking methods.

Strategy One: Broken Links

The broken link strategy is one not many businesses use, but it can have a substantial impact on SEO and search rankings [145]. It is another way of offering value, in exchange for value. However, it may even be better than a link swap. There is no need to host an outbound link and direct visitors back off the website.

The idea is simple. Perform a search for broken links on authority websites. They are common because there are all kinds of ways for a link to become dysfunctional.

Usually, the platform that it directs back to is taken offline and ceases to exist. This means that the link is less than worthless. It actually has a negative effect on SEO, because Google penalizes any content which is likely to be confusing, irrelevant, or plain frustrating for users [146].

As an aside, all websites should be checking the condition of their links on a regular basis to make sure that broken ones are identified and updated quickly [147].

They should, but some don't which is why it is possible to search for websites with broken ones.

Once they are found, the crafty individual who has done the searching can contact the owner and inform them. As a way to help, they might also suggest replacing the broken link with one to their content.

It is an aggressive way to earn backlinks, but it is legitimate, and it does benefit the other party. Obviously, the secret to success is to target only websites with similar themes and topics.

Focus on finding broken links that are possible to provide a valuable and relevant replacement for in the form of a direct path back to the target content. Finding dysfunctional links is easy with the use of a tool like Check My Links for Chrome [148].

Strategy Two: Guest Posting

Guest posting is the single best way to reach new audiences. It involves writing unique content for independent blogs and websites.

The aim is always to direct attention back to the target website, but the affiliation and endorsement from another provider increase authority and trust. This technique goes beyond simple inbound links, as forging strong connections with influential blogs is fervently rewarded [149].

Google is constantly on the lookout for these digital trails; these snaking, winding paths back and forth from valuable websites. High-quality content is never stale. It is always creating these connections and sparking pockets of interest in new corners of the internet.

Guest posting represents activity and life, which is what happens when content proves itself to be worthy of attention. For this reason, guest posting is a great form of on page search engine optimization.

It makes a big statement that even Google uses guest posts on its website [150]. They are not a simple thing to get right, though. It does take time and commitment. If there is no interest or determination to make guest blogs and articles engaging, there is no real point to creating them in the first place [151].

As always the content must be of the highest possible quality. The stakes are higher here because bad posts will simply get refused by external hosts or they will be rejected by their audience.

The good news is that there is an endless supply of blogs out there.

Find the ones which are a close match and work on forging connections with their creators. Whether the guest posting is natural (accepted out of a genuine interest) or manual (a post exchange), the results for search rankings can be enormous. Always focus on websites and blogs with a lot of followers who like to comment and engage with the content [152].

Strategy Three: Spy on the Rivals

Spying on internet competitors is a valid and recommended technique.

Most companies do it, and it isn't considered to be questionable in any way.

Just as the owner of a brick and mortar store might go on a reconnaissance trip to a rival shop, a content developer has the opportunity to observe successful e-commerce operations. The goal is to gather information, specifically about what they might be doing differently to rank so highly [153].

The most obvious way to collect data is to observe. Sign up for the newsletter or blog alerts and get a notification when new content is uploaded.

Scan it for ideas on theme and structure, because there may be popular posts that are easy to replicate.

When doing this, it is imperative that content is still created in a unique and manual fashion. Google will instantly penalize text that is copied word for word. Spin it, change it, and put a different angle on it [154].

The second way to gather information is to utilize one of the many monitoring tools available online. Monitor Backlinks, for example, is an easy to use program which tracks all of the inbound links directed to a particular website. Up to four websites can be tracked with this tool, and it organizes each link according to its impact and influence. Once the source of these backlinks is identified, there is nothing to stop a clever marketer from contacting the same external providers and trying to forge their own relationships [155].

In some cases, it won't work, because the provider has a firm arrangement with the rival company and will only post their links.

More often than not, they are happy to give a range of endorsements to companies which they believe can benefit their audience.

If a little link exchange is needed to sweeten the deal, so be it. Yes, it is a kind of poaching, but all is fair in the battle for the top spot. Just don't forget that you might be the target of somebody else's shrewd backlinking campaign.

Strategy Four: Infiltrate the Roundups

Many blogs and websites operate 'round up' alerts. These are newsletters and articles which feature countdowns, lists, and other cumulative content structures.

The aim is to offer readers as broad of a selection of sources as possible, while still staying true to a particular message or theme [156]. One example might be 'The 10 Best Event Planning Blogs on the Internet' or 'Top 5 Articles on Invoice Automation This Week.'

They can be a valuable asset for companies because their creators are always on the hunt for new sources. They actually want to hear from other content developers.

The only problem is that most receive a lot of interest and it is a matter of being a request which stands out in a crowd. Send a concise but friendly email explaining the nature of the company and the purpose of its content [157].

Include a link to two or three of the most popular articles or blogs. Then, keep an eye out for the next round up and see if an endorsement appears. Roundups are looked upon favorably by Google, as they represent votes of confidence from digital influencers. Plus, impressing the creators of these regular newsletters is a great way to form a mutually beneficial (and hopefully) long term relationship.

Strategy Five: Become an Expert

Online interviews are one of the newest strategies, but they are very popular right now. The process is simple. If a website can position itself as a convincing expert or authority, some blogs and external sources might want to showcase their knowledge.

For instance, a company selling cosmetics is a natural choice for interviews on which products to buy, how to apply them, and why they should be considered essential.

The trick is to craft a narrative around the knowledge. Rather than being a content developer, the interviewee becomes a 'Cosmetics Guru' or 'Beauty Expert.' There is no real deception or lie to this because there are always specific types of experts in all companies. Exploit the niche or market, identify an area which users are interested in, and offer practical, demonstrable advice and information [158].

The interview format is just an interesting way to frame what is, essentially, another method of content endorsement.

Now to turn to outbound links; the other side of the linking coin.

They are easy to understand, but they don't suit everybody. Some companies can see how giving a little bit of support back can lead to endorsements in the future. Others would rather avoid directing any attention whatsoever away from their own website [159].

However, the signs are that Google appreciates outbound links.

After all, if nobody was willing to use them, there would be no such thing as inbound links. The two are inexorably intertwined, and one feeds the other, so it doesn't make sense to refuse internal endorsements. Willingness to support and embrace other content providers shows confidence and a healthy attitude towards onpage SEO [160].

It is a recognition of the fact that denying visitors the chance to check out useful content (even if it exists elsewhere) negatively impacts their experience. Plus, there are those times when an agreed link exchange means that there is a direct benefit.

Some attention is being directed away from the target content, but it is being made up in traffic from the linked website.

The Two Types of Outbound Links

There are two types of outbound link, and the distinction between them is important.

There is the 'no-follow' link and the 'do-follow' link. The do follow link is a standard, run of the mill endorsement placed on the company website or commercial copy. It is exactly the kind of link which has been explained in detail throughout this section. There is nothing special required, and the code does not have to be altered [161]. The important thing to remember is that every do-follow link passes on a little bit of ranking 'juice' the endorsed website [162].

Authority or ranking juice is a way of representing the value of inbound and outbound links. It is helpful to think of it as link karma. Web sites do lose some when they link out to external content, but they usually get it back in the form of inbound links to their own pages [163]. It ebbs and flows and generally balances itself out, so companies tend not to worry too much about losing juice.

It means that the vast majority of outbound links are of the do follow variety. When indexing website pages, Google identifies them as an intention to share the juice. It crawls the connected content as well as the target pages because the instructions are to give recognition to both.

Crucially, there is a way to prevent Google from doing this and retain more ranking juice. It is what the no-follow link provides. Use it, and less karma is shared [164].

Most of the time, websites only use no-follow links because they want to make a connection to a very well established platform (like Twitter or Facebook). They know that it has so much traffic already that a tiny bit of extra juice isn't going to make any difference either way. On the other hand, keeping it back and being selfish with it has the potential to benefit smaller companies.

No follow links have this tag inside their codes:

rel="nofollow"

It is a tactical move, and it should really only be used in situations where the recipient of the juice isn't likely to notice.

Constantly holding out on similarly sized bloggers and other content creators only leads to isolation.

People don't want to work with companies that aren't willing to share and support the wider SEO community.

Furthermore, being generous with do follow links is a good way to please Google. It shows engagement and an appreciation for high-quality content.

Tips and Tricks for Valuable Outbound Links

The most important rule of outbound linking is quality over quantity. Regardless of how impressive the external information is visitors are going to switch off if confronted with web pages full of blue links. Besides, if every new link represents a little loss of juice, careful selection is advised. Generally, content creators should insert no more than four links per web page or article [165].

Try not to be tempted by private blog networks and so-called 'link farms,' because they are on a downward trajectory.

Google has embarked on a mission to wipe out this practice, so it isn't worth the risk of heavy penalties [166]. Link farms are groups of blogs or websites set up for the sole purpose of link swapping and artificial rank boosting.

Several blogs band together (or are created by one company) and spend all their time passing links and juice between one another.

Technically, the practice is successful, or it used to be. Now, Google is stamping down on artificial ranking manipulation and punishing websites constantly engaging with the same narrow group of providers.

The success of outbound linking lies with generosity and reciprocity. However, freedom is an essential part of the user experience. There needs to be a certain degree of trust in users and a belief that they won't just replace one website for another, like sheep directed into a pen. Give them value and believe that they will thank you for it.

A Little Word on Internal (Structural) Linking

The story of linking and its relationship to onpage SEO does not end here.

There is one more type of linking to discover.

It is distinct from inbound and outbound links because it doesn't have anything to do with external sources.

Internal linking for structure is all about improving navigation and making the user experience as smooth as possible [167]. It is basic, easy to understand, and offers a quick boost to Google rankings.

The rules are straightforward.

Instead of linking out or receiving links inwards, content developers create connections between their own pages, articles, and blogs.

In many instances, this will feel like a natural and intuitive thing to do. For example, a house cleaning company might offer many individual services as part of its broader commitment to 'clean.' It could provide carpet steaming, laundering for curtains, intensive restoration for appliances, and more.

It is a normal practice (and very helpful) to go into each service in more detail, perhaps with each keyword variation having its own separate landing page.

However, a more general description is what most users land on first, so the best place to discover these detailed pages is right there, in a concise overview. Placing a link to each service on this parent page enables visitors to pinpoint the information they need quickly [168]. This is the essence of internal linking. The goal is always to make a website feel logical.

The secret to making it work is ensuring that a natural, rational path develops between individual web pages. It won't be successful if links are placed without thought or care.

Think of it as the beginnings of a new village, with the web pages as important buildings. Over time, tracks and paths start to appear between certain pages because the traffic naturally flows in this direction.

The job of internal linking is to predict the course of these tracks and build them before users even realize they have a need for such direction.

As mentioned earlier, a high bounce rate is bad news for search rankings and SEO because it means that visitors are arriving, but they are not staying.

They are, literally, bouncing back off the website because something is displeasing them or failing to satisfy their needs. The best place to check out bounce rate is in Google Analytics data [169].

It displays a percentage, and this is the amount of people who leave without viewing any other pages. It is worth pointing out that a high bounce rate isn't always indicative of poor quality content or a badly designed website. On the contrary, it is more than possible to have a sky-high bounce rate and still produce lots of conversions and sales [170].

This particular scenario would suggest that visitors are finding what they need to make a purchase almost immediately.

They might spot a company phone number on the landing page and decide to call right away. Or, they might even take a note of the business address and visit in person. For this reason, bounce rate can be a little awkward.

For some websites, it does represent a problem; a mystery that needs to be solved and repaired.

For others, it is a frustrating thing, because it can end up negatively affecting SEO and search rankings even though the content is performing well. Sometimes, high functioning websites find themselves having to make concessions and changes that they don't necessarily need, in order to placate search engines.

This is a complicated question, as bounce rate is a measure of how long visitors feel like they need a website, rather than whether it helped them achieve their goal [171]. When bounce rate is high, and conversions are low, there is clearly something discouraging users.

To fix the problem and prevent it from affecting search engine optimization, the weakness must be identified. It could be related to drab content, clunky website design, slow loading speeds, or annoying features like pop-ups [172].

When a website is reasonably detailed and full of components, it becomes a process of elimination.

Unless it is glaringly obvious what might be putting visitors off, the best approach is to make little changes and watch how the bounce rate responds.

It is imperative that some form of monitoring is implemented. The process is pointless if nobody is keeping track of which changes are convincing users to stick around for longer.

This is where a technique known as AB testing is useful. It is fairly basic and requires no resources apart from a paper or digital log.

When a change is made to the website or content, it is noted, and its impact on bounce rate is observed. That way, there is a clear comparison between 'A' (the initial condition) and 'B' (the new condition). It only works if tweaks are made one at a time. The cause and effect must be easy to follow [173].

Eventually, a history of development emerges. It can be used to pinpoint design and content weaknesses so that future problems are solved quickly.

Without a detailed record, the process of elimination has to start over every time those visitors start interacting with the website in a less positive way.

For a while, it was hotly debated whether Google pays any attention to bounce rate, but it has since claimed that it does take it into account when judging onpage SEO [174].

1. Get Rid of the Pop Ups

In this day and age, websites simply don't need them.

Internet users find them hideously annoying, and many visitors refuse to return to pages with pop up ads or features.

The rules apply to any kind of pop up, whether it is a marketing element or not. Music which plays without warning, pop up images, and repetitive requests to join mailing lists are not appreciated [175]. They disrupt the user experience and take focus away from the quality of the content.

2. Improve the Navigation

The value of internal linking has already been discussed. It enhances the navigation of the website by creating tracks between related pages.

Rather than expecting visitors to search out specific pieces of content manually, it is helpful to give them a digital map. It is an easy way to travel between these metaphorical buildings.

The relationship between navigation and bounce rate is significant.

People quickly get frustrated if they land on an unfamiliar website and don't know where to go next. It is like arriving in a new town and, instead of being greeted by a guide as promised, they're left to wander aimlessly and waste valuable time searching for clues.

This is why internal linking and a smooth, logical arrangement of content is crucial.

3. Start Lazy Loading

The lazy loading technique is a great asset for small websites with big ideas. It is a design pattern process which delays the loading of certain web page elements until they are actually needed by the user [176]. Check out the Mashable website for one of the best examples of why and how this works.

The web pages load almost instantly, but only because the elements at the bottom (needed last) do not load at the same time. As each element can be configured to its own settings, lazy loading offers a remarkable degree of control over content and the way in which it is presented to visitors [177].

If there are images, videos, or other component requests that tend to extend loading times, put them on the backburner and let the user choose when to activate them.

4. Avoid Redirects Wherever Possible

The importance of outbound linking and sharing juice has been made pretty clear. Google doesn't like it when businesses are unwilling to contribute to the SEO community and give out endorsements to valuable content.

It wants to create an online world where good karma flows freely and ensures that, even when content developers are

helping others boost their ranking, they're feeling the
benefits on their own website.

There is an absurdly easy way to be generous and share juice, while retaining a connection to the user. Instead of inserting outbound links which immediately take visitors up and away from the target content, have them open in fresh windows [178]. While there is always a chance that some users will abandon the first site in favor of the second, many will continue to surf both platforms [179].

Always Write Engaging Content

All of the onpage SEO techniques already outlined are redundant if the bare bricks of the content aren't good enough for a foundation. If the written elements of the website are not entertaining or intellectually stimulating in some way, people won't read them. With hundreds of thousands of search entries to pick from, there is simply no need for an internet user to stick with content that does not entertain them.

This is crucial to an understanding of SEO and how Google ranks websites. High-quality content is grammatically precise, contains no typos or errors, has a strong narrative, and conveys a sense of purpose [180]. In fact, the most popular content is entirely practical. People use the internet because they want to find information or learn something fast. They should always come away from a website feeling like their visit has been a worthwhile experience [181].

One main thing letting companies down is an insistence on handling copy and content in the wrong way. Many assume that the real work of onpage SEO is all about the practical changes (the tweaks to loading speeds and the keyword research). On the other hand, technical strengths mean very little if not applied to content worth reading [182].

Copywriting is a skill, and not everybody has it. Settling for an in-house system if the core website team doesn't have the necessary experience is a bad idea. While hiring a freelancer or contractor is an additional expense to bear, the results will speak for themselves. Constructing a beautiful website or putting together flawless code is not the same as crafting a narrative powerful enough to lead a visitor right through to purchase.

In many ways, the copywriting side of running a website is the hardest part of all, because it doesn't lend itself well to analytical scrutiny. While it is easy enough to scrutinize traffic and determine whether content is satisfying visitors, it can be hard to know why this is the case. What is it about certain pieces of writing which captivate and immerse readers so effortlessly?

Ultimately, the answer is subjective. Everybody has their own way of engaging with content, so it is never completely possible to know why one article entertains and another falls flat. Logical inferences can be made, but the best approach is to put time and passion into its creation. Get to know the intended audience. Find out what their concerns are and what makes them really happy when they land on a website. Get up close and personal [183].

It is common for new businesses to do a little online poaching if they find themselves stuck for inspiration and ideas. Directly copying anything from a rival company is highly discouraged, but there is nothing suspect about checking out the competition and picking up on topics, titles, and themes that haven't been used before. Very young companies might want to go one step further and ape the style of an internet rival until they figure out their own, but it is imperative that the content is original enough to satisfy Google [184].

Four Ingredients for Great SEO Content

1. Originality

Originality is a big deal for Google. The search engine giant is aware that competing companies often monitor one another for tips and ideas, but it won't tolerate 'new' content that has clearly been lifted from an existing article. In fact, it can result in a long-lasting penalty and a long time spent at the bottom of results pages [185]. It takes a lot of time and effort to craft compelling, optimized content, so it is no surprise that some businesses look for an easy way out of the task.

They use article crawling bots to collect information from hundreds of existing articles and spin it into new ones. Or, they write one strong article and use an online duplicator to copy it in a thousand slightly different ways. They might invest their money in low-level copywriters, because they believe that, if a real person is hired to do the job, the content must automatically be high level [186]. The bad news is that there is no cheating the need for manually crafted blogs, articles, and web pages; not if they are going to please Google.

The single best way to rank highly for the quality of content is to create it with care and passion. This means original writing, from beginning to end, every time. While the theme, ideas, and structure have likely been used before, the words must be personally crafted. Whether this is the job of an outsourced copywriter or an in-house developer, the aim should always be to make content compelling, engaging, and exciting [187].

2. Strong Headlines

The importance of good headlines is easily underestimated because titles are the star of the show. Most content developers and onpage SEO experts spend a lot more time working on their H1 creations than they do their H2 straplines. Yet, it should be noted that only 20% of visitors read a whole article. On the other hand, 80% read every subheading and headline on the page [188]. This happens because many people skim pages to determine their worth, rather than immediately reading the introduction.

It means that hooking them with the headlines is a great way to drive traffic and reduce the bounce rate. Strong headlines do two things. They pull the reader in and make them curious to know more. They also provide a concise summary of the article [189]. For instance, if an article were titled '8 Amazing Snacks That You Can Make with Cauliflower,' an interesting strap or headline might be 'Who Knew That Cauliflower Could Taste as Good as French Fries.' It works because it's honest about the purpose of the article.

Cauliflower is not very exciting, but these restating it in another way will make it better. Internet audiences are especially fond of content that suggests they are being let in on a secret or being given exclusive information [190]. Use words like 'unbelievable,' 'shocking,' 'need to know,' and 'don't miss.' Don't be afraid to play on the desires, fears, or anxieties of a person, because emotion is a very powerful motivator [191]. For example, 'Five Grammatical Errors That Make You Look Stupid' is a compelling strapline. Fear of looking unintelligent is a good incentive to read.

Where appropriate, headlines, taglines, and straplines should have an actionable element [192]. Don't expect users to search for their own meaning. Tell them, in plain terms, how the content will improve their lives. Use verbs like 'enhance,' 'try,' 'create,' 'fix,' 'learn,' and 'promote.' Spell it out for them. Tell them why they need it. Just like Google, readers are looking for purpose and value. The quicker it is found, the greater the interest in the article, blog, or webpage.

3. Entertainment

As already mentioned, it can be tough to pinpoint exactly what it is that makes some content soar and other pieces fall. Nevertheless, the best way to find out is to stay close to the audience and understand what it is they want. Accuracy, originality, and purpose are all vital, but there is another ingredient which needs to be added to this formula – personality. Without some kind of flair or style, it is just another page of words among millions [193].

This is why copywriters and content creators should be encouraged to refine and develop personal quirks, signatures, and idiosyncrasies (as long as they don't interfere with the quality of the writing). There needs to be a careful balance between playfulness and form. Without moving away from proper grammar and logical structure, try to adopt a conversational tone [194].

Even on service pages, which are typically quite formal, there is room to speak directly to the reader and make them feel as if the content is being produced just for them. Dry, dull writing which reads like a DIY manual is no fun, and it doesn't feed the imagination. When writing blogs and articles, try to ask questions. Inviting and encouraging discussion is a good way to earn praise from Google because it creates activity on the page [195]. It also gives users a reason to engage with the content.

They do not leave wondering why they bothered to invest their time or what they got out of the deal. They chat, share ideas, and often reread pieces they find engaging. In some cases, they share them with friends who go on to share them with even more people. The popularity of the article snowballs and leads to a spike in traffic. It is all about getting content into the hands of the right people.

4. Regularity

Businesses and content developers should only launch blogs if they are willing to commit to them. Search engines are harsh on stale content and favor websites updated on a weekly basis. This can make things difficult for service websites, because there may be no desire to start and maintain a blog. They do not technically need one, but the problem becomes untreated, unchanged pages [196].

It is not usually practical to make edits to service and product pages, so a blog section is the best option. All online companies should give it some consideration if they haven't already established a source of fresh, renewable information. It forces search engine algorithms to regularly crawl and index the website. It means that the content is constantly being reviewed. As long as it is high quality and the onpage SEO is not too basic, it will result in consistently good results [197].

The more regular the updates, the better the performance, but it isn't feasible for many companies to post new blogs every single day. Most stick rigidly to a schedule or 3-4 new posts per week, and this actually gives readers time to digest the content and get excited about upcoming news and stories [198]. While frequency and freshness are important, don't be tempted into posting filler content just to fill the schedule. It must all be of the same quality and have the same capacity for engagement and entertainment.

The Future of Onpage SEO

The internet exists in a state of perpetual flux and change. By the time a person has glimpsed a small section, it has already started to change. It is interesting to think of it as akin to the human body, which is also in a state of constant renewal. In the same way that no two cells in the body remain the same after a seven-year period, the laws and rules which govern the internet are always getting faster, stronger, and more intelligent [199].

Google is at the helm of these developments because it handles over 90% of all the online searches completed on earth. It is focused on a number of key objectives. For example, the evolution of search terms and search language is currently progressing at a rapid rate. There is a growing preference for content which mimics natural speech patterns because technology is allowing users to move away from formal, typed queries.

The search engine is constantly making tweaks and changes because it is trying to stay one step ahead of increasingly sophisticated online tools.

With every new algorithm update, it makes it more difficult to cheat the system. If cheating isn't an option, the only thing content developers can do is go right back to the basics and focus on creating high-quality content, as Google always intended. It is an arms race of sorts, an inevitable push and pull between marketers (who are always going to find faster, more clever ways to create) and the search engines (trying to maintain a level playing field) [200].

3 Bold Predictions about the Future of SEO

1. The Death of the Website

For many years, SEO experts have been warning marketers of a great transition. They believe that the end of the traditional company website draws near [201]. These suspicions are related to the unstoppable rise of mobile content and mobile apps. With more searches performed on mobile devices than on conventional desktops, the way we access content is changing.

Users now prefer app-based experiences to browser-based ones, so it could be that SEO becomes an exclusively app orientated entity in the future. For businesses and content developers, this means a much greater emphasis on optimization. Every piece of content has to fit seamlessly together. Pages will be smaller, but quicker to load and more fluidly connected to one another.

The challenge with apps is brevity. They contain fewer words and more images. Therefore, it is imperative that the words chosen have the greatest possible value in terms of SEO. If businesses want to get ahead of the curve and start preparing for a future without traditional websites, they should invest in custom apps which allow users to access content in a number of different ways, rather than just via search results [202].

2. Consistent, Organic Algorithm Updates

The recent launch of RankBrain shows that Google has the future firmly in mind when it comes to SEO updates. The new algorithm is quite a complex affair but, in basic terms, it is designed to overhaul the way in which Google evolves. For a long time, the search engine has periodically released tweaks and updates (like Penguin and Panda) [203].

Many of these have targeted the use of keywords, in an attempt to make onpage SEO a more natural process and prevent websites from ranking highly with overstuffed pages. Others have made changes to the way the algorithms interpret searches, so that location is prioritized and users automatically receive results based on where they are in the world [204].

The difference with RankBrain is that these updates will now be made in smaller, incremental stages and as a consistent course of development, rather than individual changes. RankBrain is a learning algorithm with the ability to become better, faster, and more intelligent [205]. It is good news for content marketers because it means that future developments will be easier to adapt to and less likely to require extensive SEO overhauls.

3. Predictive Search Is Set to Explode

Predictive search is something that has made content marketers rather nervous in the past. When it first arrived on the scene, it was an exciting prospect, but it also meant a narrowing of possibilities. When users are not completely sure about what they want, they're more likely to pick less specific or relevant search results [206].

For instance, if a person is looking for information on organic food, they have a whole world of possibilities and opportunities to explore. While they might only intend to do some research and learn what the term means, there is a chance that they'll click through to a vendor or supermarket website and start browsing products anyway.

However, the chance of this is lowered if Google predicts the outcome of their search and offers a more specific entry. For example, they could type in the words 'organic food' and, instead of getting a list of commercial and educational pages, be directed to informational content only because Google auto-fills the entry with '…health benefits.'

The issue of specificity is complex for content developers and SEO strategists. On the one hand, the best way to rank highly and find the right audience is to create clear, practical content with a specific audience in mind. Yet, there will always be a percentage of traffic which originates from chance encounters and users with no clear goal. The continued development of predictive search makes the former more difficult [207].

What it does not mean is that 'chance' traffic is dead in the water. Now, marketers are turning to situation based SEO to grab opportunistic internet browsers. This means focusing on keywords which include situational terms [208]. Phrases like 'open until late,' 'adults only,' 'cocktail deals,' and 'two for one meal.' These are qualifying words which add relevance and specificity to content by highlighting common conditions and requirements.

Practical Improvements and Things to Think About

It is never too late to make improvements to the onpage SEO of a website or blog. It is usually quite simple and they are relatively small changes, particularly if optimization is already a part of content development. The exception is if on-page SEO has never been considered before. It might be easier to start from scratch in this case and overhaul the look and style of web pages.

The following tips are useful for both experienced and amateur content marketers.

Once the basics are grasped, search engine optimization stops being a complex behemoth with a thousand different faces.

At its heart, every strategy and technique is simple. Focus on the overarching objectives, and it becomes easier to understand them. The mistake that many businesses make is to pour money and time into tactics that work differently but, ultimately, do exactly the same thing.

Remember that all SEO techniques are designed to help content rank highly on search engine results pages.

They take different approaches, but the outcome is the same. It is the job of the content marketer to find out which ones offer the most efficient path to this end goal.

It requires commitment and willingness to adapt and change. The needs of the content won't stay the same, so a long-term outlook is needed [209].

For new companies especially, patience really is a virtue. While the internet does move at breakneck speed, it takes time for Google to pick up on changes. When carrying out AB tests and making tweaks to content, it is important to allow enough time for a response.

Don't make a change, monitor traffic for two days, and then consider the update unsuccessful because there is no immediate spike.

The best way to track the impact of changes is to log every tweak made to the website design or content. If an extensive record of developments is kept (time, date, technical changes), it becomes easier to implement multiple updates. Monitoring and reviewing their progress becomes a consistent task. Make the change, decide the length of the trial, check analytics data once it has ended [210].

Speaking of analytics, it is imperative that a solidly reliable system is used right from the start. Google Analytics is the most obvious choice, but it isn't the only option. There are scores of free and premium tools out there. All good analytics tools monitor the following six metrics; bounce rate, numbers of visitors (with a focus on unique users), referrals, exit pages, conversion rate, and most frequently visited pages [211].

Bounce rate has been covered extensively in previous sections. It measures the number of visitors who land on the first page and then immediately leave. It is impossible for websites to reduce a bounce rate to zero, but it should be kept as low as possible. The number of visitors is important for two reasons. The first is that it provides the most basic assessment of how popular the site is at any time. The second is that it distinguishes between unique visitors (new people) and existing users who are visiting the site on multiple occasions [212].

The referral metric reveals, specifically, where traffic is originating. It is a great way to confirm the value and impact of inbound links. If a lot of traffic is coming from an affiliated external source, it is clear that placing a link there was a good idea. The exit page metric is often confused with bounce rate, but the two are distinct and equally important. While bounce rate measures the number of people who land and do not move to any other pages, an 'exit page' is the place where a visitor leaves.

The content most frequently marked as 'exit pages' is where most visitors decide that the website isn't right for them or that they have had enough of engaging with it.

Clearly, people have to exit somewhere, so being the last viewed page doesn't necessarily indicate a problem. However, it is worth taking a closer look at any pages which have a much higher exit rate than the others, because there could be something turning users off.

Finally, the conversion rate is a measure of how many visitors fulfilled the objective of the website. For e-commerce platforms, this is a complete online purchase. It doesn't always have to relate to buying products, though. It could be convincing users to sign up to the mailing list or fill out an inquiry form. It could even be leading them to a particular page on the website and having them stay there long enough to fully engage with it.

Not all websites have a sitemap, but they are useful when it comes to helping Google index and categorize content.

They are also a handy tool for some visitors because not all users like to navigate content on instinct alone. Some prefer to head directly to a list of pages and pick the most relevant to their original search.

Most websites won't have more than a hundred pages, so size shouldn't be a problem. In the event that a platform is very large, it is best to create two sitemap pages.

The rule of thumb is no more than a hundred links per map (ideally, stick to 75). Otherwise, it becomes a tedious exercise in scrolling and searching, rather than a fast, practical navigation tool.

The most important lesson of all and the one which SEO strategists and content marketers should keep coming back to is that the user is king.

While Google and the other search engines have pretty powerful technologies and a lot of influence over websites, they exist to serve the user. Everything that is created for a web page must be useful to visitors in some way.

It is this level of usefulness which determines where pages appear in the results. To forget this is to condemn content to a lowly status and a poor ranking because SEO is merely a means to an end. It is a technical way for a digital entity to assess rather abstract criteria.

Value, relevance, authority, and trust are only achieved with care and attention to detail. Don't forget the end goal or the target audience.

The future belongs to those who can do more than just exploit clever SEO tricks.

It needs to be organic and instinctive. Talented content developers are able to adopt it as second nature.

This is how they create blogs and articles that sound personable, funny, warm, and entertaining. It is crucial that the focus remains with the user. After all, they are the reason the website exists.

First step is to secure a reliable domain and hosting provider; I used to use Godaddy, but have moved to Linode, which in my opinion is the fastest host available.

You can use my referral link and get started. If you decide to use Linode, you will need to most likely outsource to a developer to get going. If you need to hire a developer, you can contact me at dan@digitalmarketingwebdesign.com.

This tutorial is set up for Godaddy.

Next step is to brainstorm your domain name and begin searching for it.

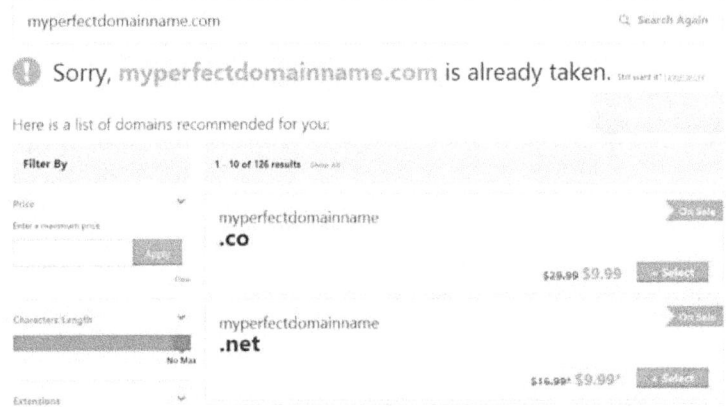

Over 1,000 websites are created a day, so it can get very competitive when trying to find the right domain name.

However, if you are lucky it will be available, remember do not just make up any name, put thought behind the **process** and **brand** you are creating!

The website domain name you pick will ultimately hopefully represent your brand and vision.

After a lot of thought and trying different domain names, you will have your **perfect domain name**.

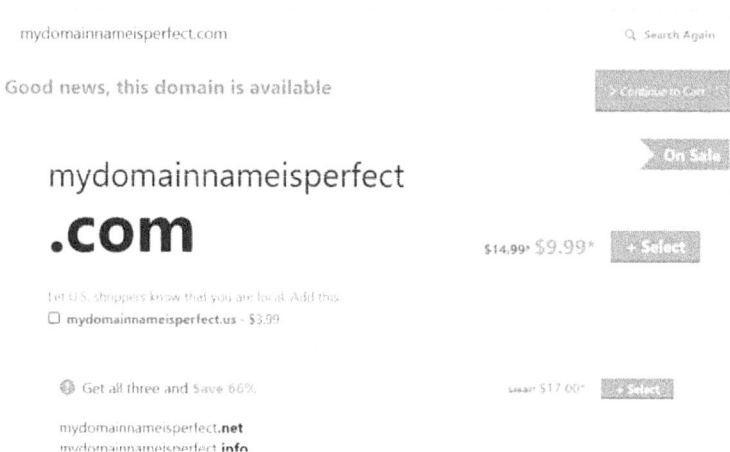

From there, get a coupon and cash back for whatever domain provider you decided on and check out!

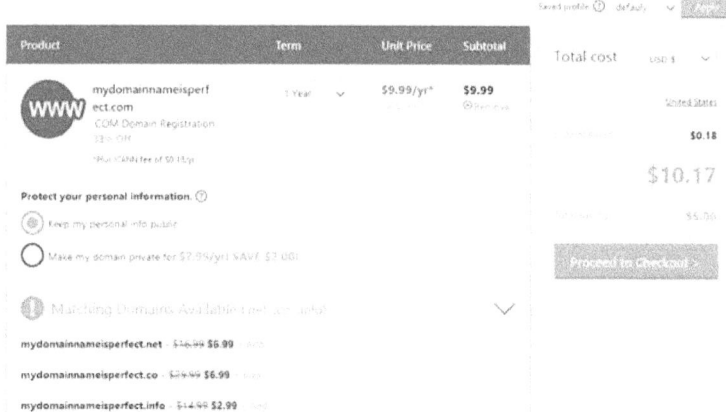

Now be patient and wait for your domain to be available on your account (typically within the hour).

The next step is to secure your web hosting; the process is pretty much the same. Select what works best for you; the budget plan should work for now. If you plan on having more than one website in the very near future, select your plan accordingly.

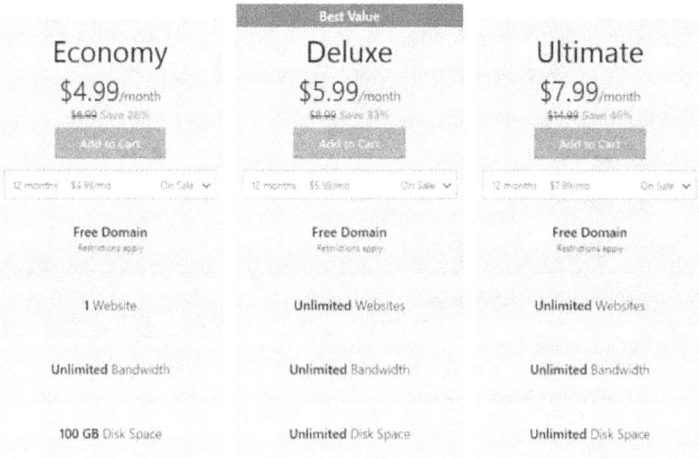

Configuring Your Web Hosting and Domain

Now once your web hosting and domain name is set up, it is time to put your domain name with your hosting.

This will be shown through Godaddy just as the above examples were.

Click Web Hosting, follow the instructions, and set up your new web hosting product so you can launch it.

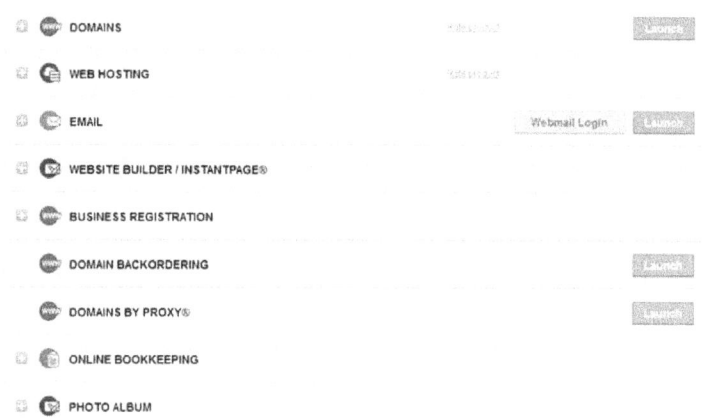

After that is done, launch it. After it loads, you will be on your dashboard screen for your web hosting.

You will see a basic screenshot of everything at a glance

Click where it says hosted domains.

Account Snapshot

Billing   Ultimate Secure

FTP Users

Applications

Databases

Hosted Domains   Domains

Email   Accounts

Bandwidth

Disk Space

You will be redirected to the hosting control center, which shows
all the domains currently on this hosting plan. You should have
0, but if you are just using this for reference then you may see
some available on there.

Click Add Domain

A window will appear for you to add your domain and folder. Type the first 3 letters of your domain and it will come up below and select it from the list. The next step is very important, you will make its folder, I recommend using something easy as it is CASE SENSITIVE, so A and a are not the same!

Add Domain

- Domain
  Bulk

Adding a domain to this hosting account lets visitors access your content through a new URL. Deluxe and Premium plans can point an added domain to any new or existing subdirectory or nested subdirectory. To point this domain to the root (*/*), leave the default Folder setting. Economy plans can point to the root, only.

Domain   Folder

| | / | Browse... |

OK   Cancel

After you choose your folder name hit OK. Make sure you write down or save your folder name, you will need it later!

You have successfully added your first domain to your hosting!

Now if everything goes alright on your hosts end, you should see it added within the next 1-24 hours.

Once your domain is added we will go back and launch our web hosting again.

Installing and Configuring WordPress

Log into Godaddy, select your web hosting and click Launch.

Once there, you will be back at your dashboard, be sure to click the hosted domains tab, and be sure that your domain is indeed added.

You will see under status it will say setup or setup primary, which means it's ready to go!

Navigate back to your dashboard. We are going to be using WordPress to make your first E-commerce website, it is by far the easiest to use and utilize for beginners and pros alike!

You will also see this below the snapshots. Click WordPress

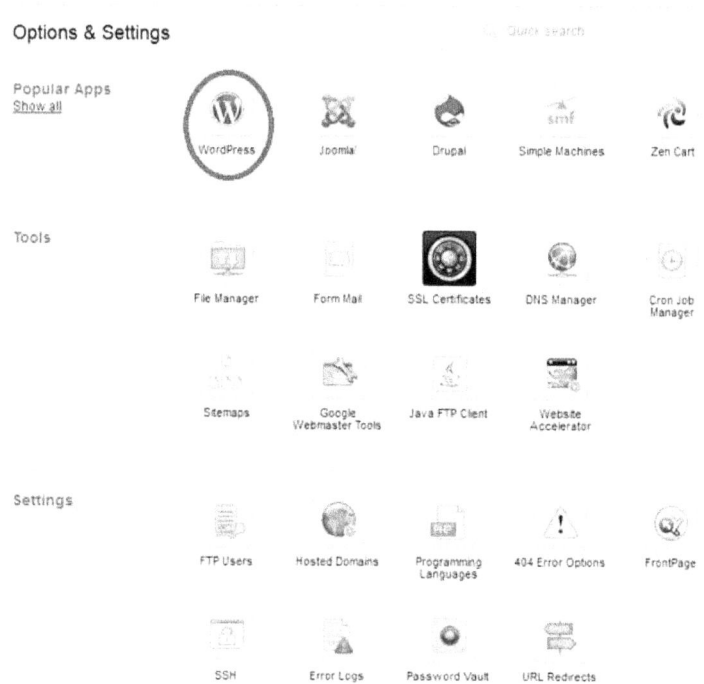

The following screen will appear.

Make sure you put in your domain name and the directory you original saved your domain name to on your web hosting!

Save the information somewhere safe, you will need it later! Not only that, but you do want to know how to access your website.

After you filled out all the details required, select OK.

While WordPress installs, utilize your time to find a WordPress theme and a few plugins to start off.

Plugins and Themes Needed

Download all of these zip files and place them in a folder you will remember.

DO NOT UNZIP the files, they will be uploaded zipped!

Woocommerce

W3 Total Cache

WP Edit

Yoast SEO

Next we want to get our theme for our website, it has to be woo commerce compatible, I recommend Elegant Themes, however if you are going for free, then go here and pick one of the available themes.

WooThemes

Save it in the same folder as the plugins.

Hopefully, by now WordPress is fully installed on your website and you have received an email telling you how to log in with a link. Click the link and bookmark it, enter in your login information and login.

You will be redirected to your admin dashboard for your website!

Once there on your left sidebar is a bunch of different tabs, which can be overwhelming at first, but you will learn how to successfully navigate your admin panel in no time!

Wordpress Dashboard – Clear Default Posts and Page

You will not be seeing the WooCommerce or Products tab yet, as you still have to upload your plugins.

First things first, click posts and delete the general post that says Hello World. This is done by hovering below the title and selecting trash, don't forget to empty your trash!

After that, click pages, and delete the sample page.

From there, you will then hover over the plugins tab and select add new.

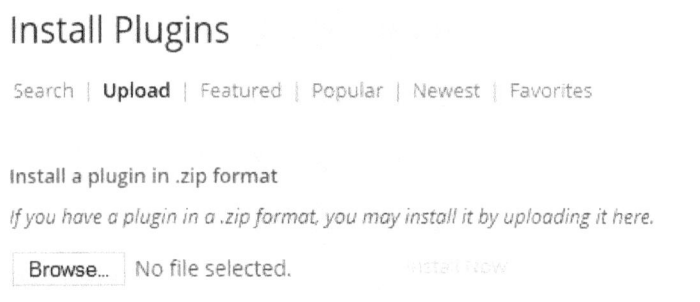

Click Upload

Install Plugins

Search | **Upload** | Featured | Popular | Newest | Favorites

Install a plugin in .zip format

If you have a plugin in a .zip format, you may install it by uploading it here.

Browse... No file selected.

Click Browse and upload a plugin, (you can only upload one at a time) after successfully uploading it, you will be redirect to a screen, be sure to click activate this plugin; otherwise it will not be active.

Do this until you have uploaded all of your plugins and successfully activated them; remember this is not where you upload your new theme at!

Now that you have successfully installed and activated your plugins, you are ready to go ahead and upload your woocommerce compatible theme you selected!

Click on appearance or hover over it to open the secondary menu.

Click Themes

You will see the following, plus your current default theme.

Themes **4**   Add New   Search installed themes...

Click **Add New**

Just as you did with the plugins, you will do the same here.

Click Upload

Install Themes

Search | Upload | Featured | Newest | Recently Updated

Search for themes by keyword.

	Search

Click Browse and add the theme!

Install Themes

Search | **Upload** | Featured | Newest | Recently Updated

Install a theme in .zip format

If you have a theme in a .zip format, you may install it by uploading it here.

Browse... No file selected.   Install Now

Upon successful completion you will be redirected to a similar page like the plugins and make sure you click activate this theme!

Setting Up Your WooCommerce Cart

Navigate to the WooCommerce part of your dashboard and select settings.

Begin filling in your store information.

Click each tab up at the top and fill in the information.

Now when you reach Checkout it is time to add your Paypal information.

| General | Products | Tax | **Checkout** | Shipping | Accounts | Emails |

Checkout Options | PayPal | BACS | Cheque | Cash on Delivery | Mijireh Checkout | CoinPayments.net

Checkout Process

Coupons   ☑ Enable the use of coupons

Coupons can be applied from the cart and checkout pages.

Checkout   ☑ Enable guest checkout

Allows customers to checkout without creating an account.

☐ Force secure checkout

Force SSL (HTTPS) on the checkout pages (an SSL Certificate is required).

Checkout Pages

These pages need to be set so that WooCommerce knows where to send users to checkout.

Cart Page   Cart   ✕ ▾

Checkout Page   Checkout   ✕ ▾

Click PayPal

The following page will appear.

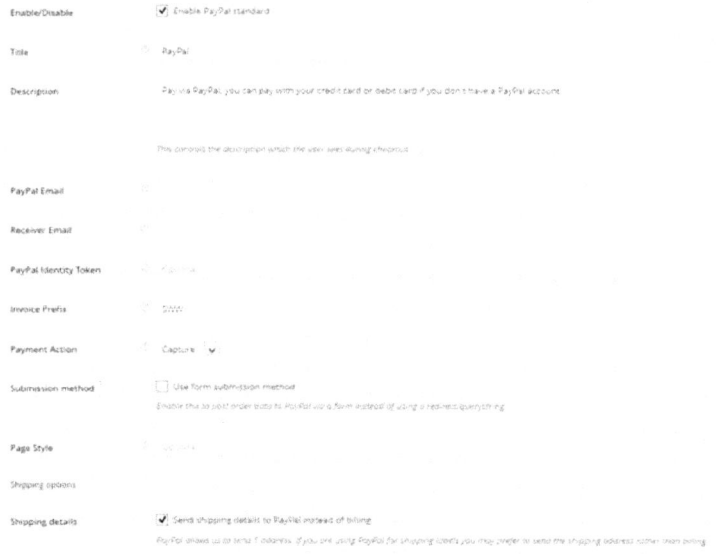

Fill in the details. Then click save.

Next click the shipping tab. It is best to just use free shipping and build the costs into your merchandise prices.

However, there are a variety of options and customizations that you can make later on down the road.

Now that we have set up every aspect of our cart, we are ready to add our products!

Adding Products to Your Website

Navigate to your wordpress admin panel.
(http://[mywebsite.com]/wp-admin)

Important, if you plan on having categories, be sure to add categories first. To do this, hover over the products tab and select categories.

Product categories for your store can be managed here. To change the order of categories on the front-end you can drag and drop to sort them. To see more categories listed click the "screen options" link at the top of the page.

Add New Product Category

Name

The name is how it appears on your site.

Slug

The "slug" is the URL-friendly version of the name. It is usually all lowercase and contains only letters, numbers, and hyphens.

Parent

None ⌄

Description

All you have to do is enter in the name of the category and click add, it will fill in the rest.

After you add your categories, hover to the products tab below WooCommerce and select add product.

You will see the following screen.

The name of your product goes up top.

The description of your product goes below.

Note your product categories for you to select from, as well as the ability to preview your product posting as you work on it.

Once you add this information, the next step is to add the product featured image.

The product image tab is your featured image, so you upload the main picture to it.

The other is the product gallery for any additional photos.

You use the product tags to add descriptive tags about you item such as blue t shirt, or the brand.

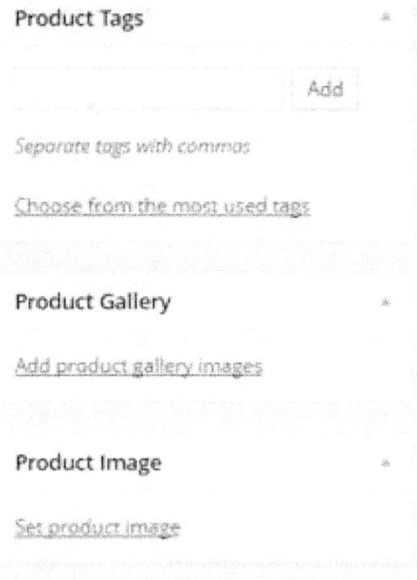

After that it is time to configure your products price and quantity.

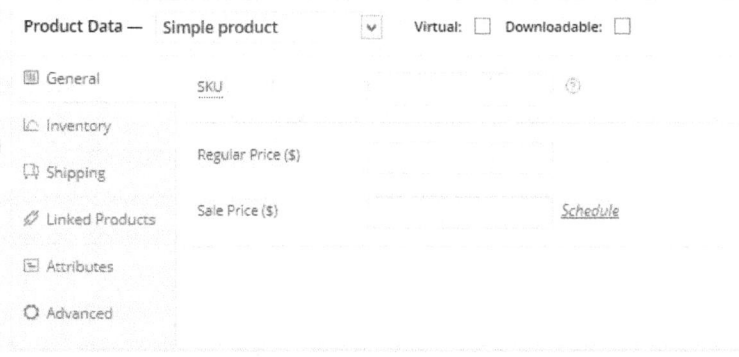

Select simple product.

Enter the regular price and sale price, or just the regular price if you want.

Click the inventory tab, set your inventory. Do the same for shipping if you plan to charge for it.

You can also link products; it will also do that for you automatically.

From there, scroll up and click Publish.

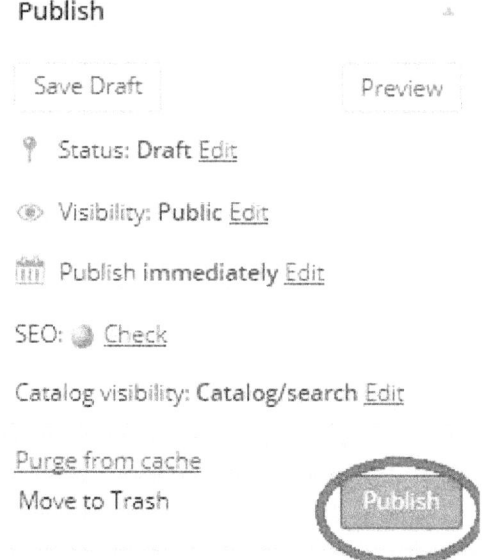

Congratulations, you have successfully created your first website and launched your first product!
Keep taking action and growing your business!

[1] Olonisakin, Bola (January 21, 2015) '4 Reasons Why Not Investing in Web Presence Is a Dumb Idea' http://www.gtechdesigns.com/4-reasons-why-not-investing-in-web-presence-is-a-dumb-idea/

[2] Mills, Ian (September 2, 2015) 'Five Reasons Website Traffic is the Lifeblood of Small Businesses' http://www.huffingtonpost.com/ian-mills/5-reasons-website-traffic_b_6628080.html

[3] Martin, James (December 22, 2009) '5 SEO Secrets to make Your Site More Visible' http://www.pcworld.com/article/185251/seo_secrets_search_engine_optimization.html

[4] Paul, Ross (June 26, 2015) 'Just How Big is the E-Commerce Market?' http://blog.lemonstand.com/just-how-big-is-the-ecommerce-market-youll-never-guess/

[5] Anderson, Shaun (February 4, 2017) 'How to Get Number One on Google Without Breaking the Rules' http://www.hobo-web.co.uk/how-to-get-to-number-1-on-google/

[6] Broer Rolf (December 8, 2011) 'Search Engine Algorithm Basics' http://www.hobo-web.co.uk/how-to-get-to-number-1-on-google/

[7] Sean (July 31, 2015) '10 Things Google Hates about Your Website' https://www.wolfgangdigital.com/blog/badvertisement-10-things-google-hates-about-your-website/

[8] Chris, Alex (Retrieved February 13, 2016) 'What Is Off Page SEO?' https://www.reliablesoft.net/what-is-off-page-seo/

[9] Patel, Neil (Retrieved February 13, 2016) 'The On Page SEO Cheat Sheet' http://neilpatel.com/blog/the-on-page-seo-cheat-sheet/

[10] Dean, Brian (October 8, 2016) 'On Page SEO: Anatomy of a Perfectly Optimised Page' http://backlinko.com/on-page-seo

[11] Shelley, Ryan (October 18, 2016) '3 Things to Do After a Major Google Algorithm Update' http://searchengineland.com/3-things-major-google-algorithm-update-260828

[12] Morrow, Jon (August 31, 2016) '6 SEO Mistakes That Will Make Google Hate You Forever' https://smartblogger.com/seo-mistakes/

[13] Louis, Daniel (Retrieved on February 23, 2017) '13 Super Easy Ways to Immediately Improve Your SEO' http://www.jeffbullas.com/2016/03/29/13-super-easy-ways-to-immediately-improve-your-seo-ranking/

[14] Steimle, Josh (September 12, 2013) 'What Does SEO Cost?' https://www.forbes.com/forbes/welcome/?toURL=https://www.forbes.com/sites/joshsteimle/2013/09/12/what-does-

seo-cost-
infographic/&refURL=https://www.google.co.uk/&referrer
=https://www.google.co.uk/

[15] Speakman, Porter (July 14, 2014) 'Google's Battle for
Authenticity'
http://www.uzu-media.com/blog/Googles-Battle-for-
Authenticity

[16] Alton, Larry (July 29, 2015) '7 Ways to Make Your
Brand More Authentic on Social Media'
https://socialmediaweek.org/blog/2015/07/more-authentic-
brands/

[17] Apostolovski, Dim (Retrieved on February 27, 2017)
'What Are Backlinks and Why Are They Important for
SEO?'
https://www.wmegroup.com.au/seo/what-are-backlinks-
why-are-they-important-for-seo/

[18] Demaria, Boris (April 20, 2013) 'What Id PageRank
and Why Is It Important in 2013?'
https://www.woorank.com/en/blog/what-is-pagerank

[19] Chris, Alex (Retrieved on February 27, 2017) '10 Bad SEO Practices That Will Destroy Your Google Rankings' https://www.reliablesoft.net/10-bad-seo-practices-that-will-destroy-your-google-rankings/

[20] Halimi, Natalie (January 21, 2014) 'Good SEO is Natural Content Management' https://www.similarweb.com/blog/good-seo-is-natural-content-management

[21] De Vaak, Joost (May 25, 2016) 'Crafting Good Titles for SEO' https://yoast.com/page-titles-seo/

[22] Simpson, Jack (September 14, 2015) 'Why Visitors Only Read 20% of Your Webpage' https://econsultancy.com/blog/66920-why-visitors-only-read-20-of-your-web-page/

[23] Meyers, Peter (February 23, 2011) 'I'm Ranking, So Where Is My Traffic?'
https://moz.com/blog/im-ranking-wheres-my-traffic

[24] Chris, Alex (Retrieved on February 27, 2017) 'How to Write SEO Friendly Content'
https://www.reliablesoft.net/how-to-write-seo-friendly-content/

[25] Patel, Neil (Retrieved on February 29, 2017) '10 Advanced SEO Techniques That Will Double Your Search Traffic'
http://neilpatel.com/blog/10-advanced-seo-techniques-thatll-double-your-search-traffic/

[26] Bellis, Stuart (March 17, 2017) 'How to Write SEO Friendly Title Tags and Meta Descriptions'
http://www.code7.co.uk/blog/how-to-write-seo-friendly-title-tags-and-meta-descriptions

[27] Wheeler, Aaron (September 29, 2011) 'Title Tags: Is 70 Characters the Best Practice?'
https://moz.com/blog/title-tags-is-70-characters-the-best-practice-whiteboard-friday

[28] Slegg, Jennifer (May 16, 2016) 'New Mobile Title Tag Lengths for Google Search Results' http://www.thesempost.com/google-mobile-title-tag-length/

[29] Churt, Rebecca (February 19, 2014) 'How to Optimise Your Page Titles for Mobile Search' https://blog.hubspot.com/marketing/how-to-optimize-page-titles-mobile-search-quick-tip

[30] Miffsud, Justin (October 3, 2011) '15 Title Tag Optimisation Guidelines for SEO' http://usabilitygeek.com/15-title-tag-optimization-guidelines-for-usability-and-seo/

[31] Anderson, Shaun (February 4, 2017) 'SEO Tutorial for Beginners in 2017' http://www.hobo-web.co.uk/seo-tutorial/

[32] Gunelius, Susan (February 6, 2017) 'Tricks to Use Keyword In Your Blog Posts'

https://www.lifewire.com/tricks-to-use-keywords-in-blog-posts-3476654

[33] Oprea, Eugen (March 18, 2014) '10 Steps a Local Business Can Take Today to Improve Search Rankings' http://www.copyblogger.com/local-seo/

[34] Reisenwitz, Cathy (October 9, 2014) 'Should I Name My Products with Keywords?' http://blog.capterra.com/product-name-seo-name-products-keywords/

[35] Lee, Kevan (March 31, 2014) 'The Ideal Length of Everything Online, Backed By Research' https://blog.bufferapp.com/the-ideal-length-of-everything-online-according-to-science

[36] Birkner, Christine (November, 2015) 'Six SEO Rules for 2016' https://www.ama.org/publications/MarketingNews/Pages/seo-rules-2016.aspx

[37] dijola, Victor (July 29, 2015) 'Why Infographics are the Secret to Super SEO' https://thenextweb.com/insider/2015/07/29/why-infographics-are-the-secret-to-super-seo/#.tnw_F2xshx2U

[38] Hodgdon, Michael (March 9, 2015) 'What Is Flickr and Why You Should Be Using It to Help Your SEO' http://www.infront.com/blogs/the-infront-blog/2015/9/3/flickr-for-seo

[39] Stanley, Tim (February 24, 2017) 'The Importance of High Quality, Original, Focused Content' https://onward.justia.com/2017/02/24/importance-high-quality-original-focused-content/

[40] Gardiner, Marie (May 11, 2016) 'What to Do When Your Images Are Used Without Permission' https://photography.tutsplus.com/articles/what-to-do-when-your-images-are-used-without-permission--cms-26465

[41] Rouse, Margaret (Retrieved March 3, 2017) 'Lossless and Lossy Compression' http://whatis.techtarget.com/definition/lossless-and-lossy-compression

[42] Hayes, Mark (Retrieved March 3, 2017) '10 Must Know Image Optimisation Tips' https://www.shopify.co.uk/blog/7412852-10-must-know-image-optimization-tips

[43] Halpern, Derek (Retrieved March 1, 2017) 'How to Optimize Images for Better Search Engine Rankings' http://diythemes.com/thesis/wordpress-seo-image-optimization/

[44] Fernandez, Chris (March 21, 2012) 'Website Image Usability and SEO Best Practices' http://usabilitygeek.com/website-image-usability-and-seo-best-practices/

[45] Boudreaux, Ryan (April 14, 2011) 'Tips for Optimizing Your Web Images' http://www.techrepublic.com/blog/web-designer/tips-for-optimizing-your-web-images/

[46] Dion, Jean (July 21, 2015) 'SEO 101: Optimise Your Images and Make Them SEO Rock Stars' https://www.searchenginejournal.com/seo-101-optimize-images-make-seo-rockstars-4-steps/136290/

[47] Rieckmann, Jay (March 14, 2013) 'Keyword Research Is the Most Important Part of SEO' http://www.thrivecreativelabs.com/blog/2013-03-14-why-keyword-research-most-important-seo-element

[48] Patel, Neil (Retrieved March 1, 2017) 'The Ultimate Google Algorithm Cheat Sheet' http://neilpatel.com/blog/the-ultimate-google-algorithm-cheat-sheet/

[49] Traphagen, Mark (August 8, 2016) 'The Three Pillars of SEO: Authority Relevance and Trust' https://www.searchenginejournal.com/seo-guide/search-authority/

[50] Gregorio, Jomer (January 29, 2015) 'Keyword Research: How It Works and Why Is It Important'

http://cjgdigitalmarketing.com/keyword-research-how-it-works-and-why-it-is-important/

[51] Kolowich, Lindsay (March 29, 2016) 'The 9 Best Keyword Research Tools to Find the Right Keywords for SEO' https://blog.hubspot.com/blog/tabid/6307/bid/22842/4-Helpful-Tools-for-Identifying-the-Right-Keywords.aspx

[52] Isca, Frank (June 4, 2013) 'Keyword Research Tips for Local Businesses' https://www.weidert.com/whole_brain_marketing_blog/bid/116092/Geographic-SEO-Keyword-Research-Tips-for-Local-Businesses

[53] Gavril, Alexandra (February 1, 2016) 'Why Keywords Are Still Important In 2016' https://www.123-reg.co.uk/blog/seo-2/why-keywords-are-still-important-in-2016/

[54] 'Virji, Purna (May 5, 2016) 'How Voice Search Will Change Digital Marketing for the Better' https://moz.com/blog/how-voice-search-will-change-digital-marketing-for-the-better

[55] Picone, Giovanni (Retrieved March 1, 2017) 'Semantics Search, SEO, and Making Google More Human' https://www.electricdialogue.com/semantic-search-seo-making-google-human/

[56] Patel, Neil (Retrieved March 1, 2017) 'Everything You Need to Know about Semantic Search and What It Means for Your Website' https://www.crazyegg.com/blog/everything-about-semantic-search/

[57] Fishkin, Rand (August 19, 2016) 'When and How to Listen to Google's Public Statements about SEO' https://moz.com/blog/when-and-how-to-listen-to-googles-public-statements-about-seo-whiteboard-friday

[58] Perez, Sarah (July 28, 2015) 'Recent App Store Algorithm to Crackdown on Keyword Stuffing'

https://techcrunch.com/2015/07/28/report-recent-app-store-algorithm-change-points-to-crackdown-on-keyword-stuffing/

[59] Parsons, Chris (Retrieved March 2, 2017) 'SEO 101: Understanding Google's Algorithms' http://www.rippleffect.com/news-views/seo-101-understanding-googles-algorithms/

[60] Siu, Eric (January 20, 2014) 'Is Your SEO Strategy Ready for Google's New Algorithm?' https://www.entrepreneur.com/article/230898

[61] Charlton, Graham (December 2, 2015) 'The Importance of User Reviews for Local SEO' https://searchenginewatch.com/sew/how-to/2436136/the-importance-of-user-reviews-for-local-seo

[62] Agrawal, Harsh (March 21, 2017) '5 Excellent Websites for Checking Google Keyword Rankings https://www.shoutmeloud.com/5-excellent-websites-to-

check-keyword-ranking-in-google.html

[63] Anastasia (July 22, 2015) 'How to Identify and Analyse Keywords Your Competitors Are Using' https://www.cleverism.com/how-to-identify-analyze-keywords-competitors-are-using/

[64] Churt, Rebecca (March 26, 2013) 'How to Conduct a Competitive SEO Audit to Outrank Industry Rivals' https://blog.hubspot.com/marketing/how-to-conduct-competitive-seo-audit

[65] Mothner, Michael (Retrieved March 2, 2017) '5 Secrets to Selecting Highly Effective SEO Keywords' http://www.inc.com/guide/2010/06/picking-effective-seo-keywords.html

[66] Kumar, AJ (October 25, 2012) '5 Ways to Beat Your Competitors at SEO' https://www.entrepreneur.com/article/224785

[67] Wilson, Nolan (February 13, 2013) 'How to Naturally Integrate Keywords Into Your Online Content' http://www.benchmarkemail.com/blogs/detail/how-to-naturally-integrate-keywords-into-your-online-content

[68] Fitzgerald, Harry (February 25, 2015) 'What Is the Ideal SEO Keyword Density?' http://www.silver-monkey.co.uk/what-is-the-ideal-seo-keyword-density/

[69] Fishkin, Rand (October 24, 2014) 'A Visual Guide to Keyword Targeting and On Page SEO' https://moz.com/blog/visual-guide-to-keyword-targeting-onpage-optimization

[70] Deelstra, Keesjan (2 September, 2010) 'Adding Keywords to Your Website' https://www.seoeffect.com/blog-en/seo-tips-and-tricks-posts/text-component-adding-keywords-web-site/

[71] Agrawal, Harsh (January 8, 2016) 'What's the Optimum Keyword Density for Better Ranking?' https://www.shoutmeloud.com/keyword-density-seo.html

[72] Sukhraj, Ramona (May 22, 2015) 'The 3 Most Important Things You Need to Know about SEO for SaaS' https://www.impactbnd.com/blog/the-3-most-important-things-you-need-to-know-about-seo-for-saas

[73] Burton, Robin (January 27, 2009) 'Why You Need a Dedicated Landing Page https://seositecheckup.com/articles/why-you-need-a-dedicated-landing-page

[74] Mahaney, Stephen (Retrieved March 2, 2017) '3 Good Reasons to Target Long Tail Keywords' https://www.wordtracker.com/academy/keyword-research/technical-guides/three-good-reasons-to-target-long-tail-keywords

[75] Demers, Jayson (June 25, 2015) 'Why Local SEO Is about to Become Even More Important' https://www.entrepreneur.com/article/247515

[76] Narayan, Hari (May, 5, 2016) 'How to Write SEO Friendly Post Title for More Blog Traffic?' https://www.shoutmeloud.com/how-to-write-seo-friendly-post-title.html

[77] Wainright, Corey (November 17, 2011) 'The Ultimate Guide for Mastering Long Tail Search' https://blog.hubspot.com/blog/tabid/6307/bid/28912/The-Ultimate-Guide-for-Mastering-Long-Tail-Search.aspx

[78] Donovan, John (March 12, 2014) 'Beginners Guide: Advantages of Targeting Long Tail Keywords' http://www.lunametrics.com/blog/2014/03/12/beginners-guide-longtail-keywords/

[79] Halliur, Akshay (January 19, 2017) 'How to Find LSI Keywords and Smartly Implement Them for SEO' https://www.gobloggingtips.com/lsi-keywords/

[80] Singla, Ankit (Retrieved March 4, 2017) 'How to Find LSI Keywords and Use Them to Boost SEO Traffic?' https://www.bloggertipstricks.com/lsi-keywords.html

[81] Virgillito, Dan (August 18, 2014) 'LSI Keywords Can Help Your Content Rank Faster' http://www.webhostingsecretrevealed.net/blog/seo/lsi-keywords-can-help-your-content-rank-faster/

[82] Agrawal, Harsh (February 27, 2017) 'Awesome Free SEO Keyword Suggestion Tool' https://www.shoutmeloud.com/ubersuggest-awesome-free-seo-keyword-suggestion-tool.html

[83] Weinstein, Mindy (August 5, 2016) 'How to Know Your Audience to Master Your Marketing Campaigns'

https://www.searchenginejournal.com/seo-guide/know-your-audience/

[84] Jain, Gaurav (January 31, 2017) 'H1 and H2 Heading Tags for SEO'
http://www.emoneyindeed.com/h1-h2-heading-tags-seo-use/

[85] Fergusson, Bill (January 26, 2016) 'The SEO Title Tag'
https://www.brightedge.com/blog/the-seo-title-tag/

[86] Ratcliff, Christopher (May 16, 2016) 'How to Write Meta Title Tags for SEO'
https://searchenginewatch.com/2016/05/16/how-to-write-meta-title-tags-for-seo-with-good-and-bad-examples/

[87] Purtell, Marc (Retrieved March 4, 2017) 'How Important Is an H1 Tag for SEO?'
https://www.searchenginejournal.com/in-2014-how-important-is-an-h1-tag-for-seo/

[88] Anderson, Shaun (January 22, 2016) 'How to Use H1-H6 HTML Elements Properly'
http://www.hobo-web.co.uk/headers/

[89] Jones, Duncan (September 16, 2010) 'H1, H2 and H3 Header Tags for SEO'
https://www.tmprod.com/blog/2010/h1-h2-and-h3-header-tags-for-seo/

[90] Barysevich, Aleh (February 27, 2016) 'How Important Are Tags in 2016 for SEO?'
https://www.searchenginejournal.com/important-tags-2016-seo/156440/

[91] Franco, Andy (October 29, 2015) 'The Dos and Don'ts to Using Header Tags for SEO'
https://www.v9seo.com/blog/2015/10/29/the-dos-and-donts-to-using-header-tags-for-seo/

[92] Kelly, Ryan (August 18, 2014) 'How to Write a Header Tag for SEO'
http://pearanalytics.com/blog/2014/how-to-write-a-header-tag-h1-for-seo/

[93] Pilon, Annie (May 8, 2013) 'What is Responsive Web Design?'
https://smallbiztrends.com/2013/05/what-is-responsive-web-design.html

[94] Sterling, Greg (May 5, 2015) 'Google Says More Searches Now on Mobile Than On Desktop'
http://searchengineland.com/its-official-google-says-more-searches-now-on-mobile-than-on-desktop-220369

[95] Pettit, Nick (June 2, 2014) 'The 2014 Guide to Responsive Web Design'
http://blog.teamtreehouse.com/modern-field-guide-responsive-web-design

[96] Robinson, Jim (April 6, 2015) 'Mobile SEO: Responsive Design vs. Separate Mobile Site vs. Dynamic Serving
http://www.clickseed.com/responsive-design-vs-separate-mobile-site-vs-dynamic-serving/

[97] Smashing Editorial (January 12, 2011) 'Responsive Web Design: What is It and How to Use It'
https://www.smashingmagazine.com/2011/01/guidelines-for-responsive-web-design/

[98] Wood, Ben (March 31, 2015) 'Mobile SEO: Ensuring Your Website is Mobile Friendly'
https://www.hallaminternet.com/essential-guide-mobile-seo/

[99] Graham, Geoff) 'November 11, 2015) 'The Difference between Responsive and Adaptive Design'
https://css-tricks.com/the-difference-between-responsive-and-adaptive-design/

[100] Martin, James (July 6, 2016) '8 Things You Need to Know about Google AMP' http://www.cio.com/article/3091071/search/8-things-you-need-to-know-about-google-amp.html

[101] Ratcliff, Christopher (July 6, 2016) 'Is Google AMP a Ranking Signal?' https://searchenginewatch.com/2016/07/06/is-google-amp-a-ranking-signal/

[102] Little, David (Retrieved March 6, 2017) 'Understanding the Fluid Grid: Part One' https://www.littled.net/2012/01/understanding-the-fluid-grid-part-one/

[103] Storey, Dudley (Retrieved March 6, 2017) 'CSS Fluid Image Techniques for Responsive Site Design' http://thenewcode.com/586/CSS-Fluid-Image-Techniques-for-Responsive-Site-Design

[104] Heng, Christopher (Retrieved March 6, 2017) 'How to Make a Two Column Website Layout Mobile Friendly' https://www.thesitewizard.com/css/mobile-ready-two-column-layout.shtml

[105] Riddle, Ryan (Retrieved March 6, 2017) 'How to Use Media Queries in Responsive Web Design' https://www.uxpin.com/studio/blog/media-queries-responsive-web-design/

[106] Van Gemert, Vasilis (March 1, 2013) 'Logical Breakpoints for Your Responsive Design' https://www.smashingmagazine.com/2013/03/logical-breakpoints-responsive-design/

[107] Gremillion, Ben (Retrieved March 6, 2017) 'A Hands On Guide to Mobile First Design' https://www.uxpin.com/studio/blog/a-hands-on-guide-to-mobile-first-design/

[108] Edwards, Samuel (September 7, 2015) 'How to Decrease Bounce Rates with Simple Onsite Tweaks' http://www.audiencebloom.com/how-to-decrease-bounce-rates-with-simple-onsite-tweaks/

[109] Cyriac (December 24, 2008) 'How Bounce Rates Affect Your Website Rankings https://www.techwyse.com/blog/search-engine-optimization/how-bounce-rates-effect-your-website-rankings/

[110] Jackson, Brian (December 2, 2016) '16 Website Speed Test Tools for Analyzing Web Performance' https://www.keycdn.com/blog/website-speed-test-tools/

[111] Aragon, Kathryn (Retrieved March 11, 2017) '10 Ways to Speed Up Your Website' https://www.crazyegg.com/blog/speed-up-your-website/

[112] Hoffman, Billy (August 1, 2013) 'How Website Speed Actually Impacts Search Ranking'

https://moz.com/blog/how-website-speed-actually-impacts-search-ranking

[113] Taylor, Marcus (Retrieved March 12, 2017) 'How to Improve Your Page Load Speed by 70.39% in 45 Minutes' https://www.ventureharbour.com/improving-site-speed/

[114] Crystal, Gregg (August 3, 2015) '5 Easy Ways to Help Reduce Your Website's Page Loading Speed' https://blog.hubspot.com/marketing/how-to-reduce-your-websites-page-speed

[115] Laja, Peep (Retrieved March 12, 2017) '11 Low Hanging Fruits for Increasing Website Speed' https://conversionxl.com/11-low-hanging-fruits-for-increasing-website-speed-and-conversions/

[116] B, Gediminas (December 9, 2016) 'Improving Website Performance: Gzip Compression' https://www.hostinger.com/tutorials/website/improving-

website-performance-gzip-compression

[117] Sexton, Patrick (March 17, 2016) 'Leverage Browser Caching'
https://varvy.com/pagespeed/leverage-browser-caching.html

[118] Tess (March 29, 2012) 'Leverage Browser Caching: How to Add Expires Headers'
http://fortheloveofseo.com/blog/performance/leverage-browser-caching-how-to-add-expires-headers/

[119] Rouse, Margaret (Retrieved March 12, 2017) 'WYSIWYG (What You See Is What You Get)
http://whatis.techtarget.com/definition/WYSIWYG-what-you-see-is-what-you-get

[120] Olufisayo (May 23, 2015) 'Advantages and Disadvantages Offered by WYSIWYG Editors'
http://www.entrepreneurshipsecret.com/wysiwyg-editors/

[121] Hadi, Agus (July 31, 2016) 'How to Compress Javascript File Using Closure Compiler' http://webdevzoom.com/compress-javascript-file-using-closure-compiler/

[122] Emily (July 23, 2015) 'Simple SEO Tips for Boosting Site Speed' http://netvantagemarketing.com/blog/simple-seo-tips-for-boosting-site-speed/

[123] Heijmans, Michiel (February 4, 2017) 'Optimizing Images for SEO' https://yoast.com/image-seo/

[124] Nolasco da Silva, Chandal (May 17, 2016) 'SEO Best Practices When Using GIFS' https://www.searchenginejournal.com/gifs-google-good-content-bad-seo-practice/162753/

[125] de Valk, Joost (February 13, 2017) 'Image SEO: Alt Tag and Title Tag Optimization' https://yoast.com/image-seo-alt-tag-and-title-tag-optimization/

[126] Johansson, Johan (April 3, 2013) 'How to Make Your Websites Faster on Mobile Devices' https://www.smashingmagazine.com/2013/04/build-fast-loading-mobile-website/

[127] Blazej (Retrieved March 12, 2017) 'Tips to Improve SEO with Website Translation' https://www.textunited.com/blog/tips-to-improve-seo-with-website-translation/

[128] Fishkin, Rand (February 24, 2009) '5 Reasons You Should Link Out to Others from Your Website' https://moz.com/blog/5-reasons-you-should-link-out-to-others-from-your-website

[129] Ball, Jon (July 21, 2014) 'What Is Link Building?'
https://searchenginewatch.com/sew/opinion/2356174/what-is-link-building

[130] Si, Sean (Retrieved March 12, 2017) 'Outbound Links   Tutorial'
https://seo-hacker.com/outbound-links-tutorial/

[131] Patel, Neil (Retrieved March 11, 2017) '17 SEO Myths   That   You   Should   Never   Follow'
http://neilpatel.com/blog/17-seo-myths-that-you-should-never-follow/

[132] Labrador, Emma (January 28, 2016) 'Why Should You   Focus   on   Internal   Linking?'
http://positionly.com/blog/seo/internal-linking

[133] Northcutt, Corey (May 11, 2016) 'Inbound Link Building 101: 33 White Hat Ways to Build Backlinks for SEO'
https://blog.hubspot.com/blog/tabid/6307/bid/32479/32-

white-hat-ways-to-build-inbound-links.aspx

[134] Lodico, Jim (December 27, 2010) '7 Ways to Improve Your Blog SEO with Inbound Links' http://www.socialmediaexaminer.com/7-ways-to-improve-your-blog-seo-with-inbound-links/

[135] Bourn, Jennifer (November 8, 2013) '10 Ideas to Build Quality Inbound Links' http://www.bourncreative.com/10-ideas-build-inbound-links-website-traffic/

[136] Bourn, Jennifer (December 4, 2013) 'Understanding Reciprocal Links and How to Use Them' http://www.bourncreative.com/using-reciprocal-links-the-right-way/

[137] DeMers, Jayson (January 6, 2016) 'Your Guide to Link Building for SEO in 2016' https://www.forbes.com/sites/jaysondemers/2016/01/06/your-guide-to-link-building-for-seo-in-2016/#7947540c1a9b

[138] Chris, Alex (Retrieved March 11, 2017) 'What Is Natural Link Building?' https://www.reliablesoft.net/what-is-natural-link-building-examples-and-case-study/

[139] Jensen, Brian (November 7, 2013) 'The Essential Guide to Effective Link Building Outreach' http://www.buzzstream.com/blog/essential-guide-effective-link-building-outreach.html

[140] Connell, Adam (November 1, 2016) 'The Essential Guide to Link Building without Risking Your Rankings' http://www.bloggingwizard.com/link-building-in-2015/

[141] Anderson, Shaun (February 7, 2017) 'Link Building: How to Build Links to Your Website in 2017' http://www.hobo-web.co.uk/link-building-strategy-for-beginners-a-month-of-free-tips/

[142] Speyer, James (August 29, 2016) '21 Types of Dangerous, Worthless, Or Just Plain Junk Backlinks' https://exposureninja.com/21-types-dangerous-worthless-just-plain-junk-backlinks/

[143] Markey, Sean (April 6, 2016) 'How to Build Quality Backlinks By Fixing the Web' https://ahrefs.com/blog/broken-link-building/

[144] Blizzard, Trent (March 21, 2014) 'Broken Links, Pages, Images and 404s Hurt SEO' http://www.blizzardpress.com/404-errors-and-seo-rankings/

[145] Soames, Chris (September 11, 2014) '5 Essential Link Checking Tools for SEOs, Bloggers, and Content Editors' http://www.smartinsights.com/search-engine-optimisation-seo/link-building/site-link-checking-tools/

[146] Basu, Saikat (June 10, 2011) '6 Chrome Extensions That Check the Validity and Safety of Webpage Links with a Click' http://www.makeuseof.com/tag/6-chrome-extensions-check-validity-safety-webpage-links-click/

[147] Enge, Eric (May 27, 2014) 'The Indirect SEO Benefits of Guest Posting' http://searchengineland.com/indirect-seo-benefits-guest-posting-192029

[148] DeMers, Jayson (April 16, 2013) 'The Top 5 Benefits of Guest Blogging' https://www.searchenginejournal.com/the-top-5-benefits-of-guest-blogging/62256/

[149] Tanguay, Adam (January 19, 2017) 'The Winning SEO Strategy Most Bloggers Miss' http://positionly.com/blog/guest-blogging-seo-strategy

[150] Si, Sean (Retrieved March 13, 2017) 'How to Find the Best Sites for Guest Blogging' https://seo-hacker.com/find-sites-guest-blogging/

[151] Baker, Loren (August 27, 2009) 'SEO Competitive Intelligence: Learn from Your SEO Rivals' https://www.searchenginejournal.com/seo-competitive-intelligence/12816/

[152] Cope, Ben (June 22, 2016) 'Is Copying Website Content Bad for SEO?' http://thecontentworks.uk/copying-website-content-bad-seo/

[153] Robbie (June 14, 2014) 'How to Steal Your Competitor's Backlinks, Rankings, and Traffic' http://www.robbierichards.com/seo/steal-competitors-backlinks-rankings/

[154] Eric (Retrieved March 13, 2017) 'What Is Link Roundup Link Building?' https://growtheverywhere.com/seo/link-roundup-link-building-practical-guide/

[155] Soulo, Tim (Retrieved March 13, 2017) 'How to Push Your Articles to Link Roundups without Even Thinking about It' http://bloggerjet.com/link-roundups/

[156] French, Garrett (January 12, 2010) 'Link Building with Interviews: How Thought Leadership Builds Links and Leads' http://searchengineland.com/link-building-with-interviews-how-thought-leadership-builds-links-leads-33149

[157] Baldwin, Steve (Retrieved March 15, 2017) 'Fear of Linking: The Truth about Outbound Links' http://www.didit.com/fear-of-linking-the-truth-about-outbound-links/

[158] Agrawal, Harsh (December 23, 2015) 'How Outbound Link Improves Your Blog Authority and Ranking'
https://www.shoutmeloud.com/seo-benefits-and-tips-for-outbound-links.html

[159] Sudhakaran, Anoop (April 13, 2015) 'Understand Dofollow and Nofollow Link: SEO Basics'
https://www.shoutmeloud.com/understand-dofollow-nofollow-link-seo-basics.html

[160] Si, Sean (Retrieved March 15, 2017) 'Lesson 13: Outbound Links'
https://seo-hacker.com/basic-seo/lesson-13-outbound-links/

[161] Lyons, Ken (May 15, 2015) 'Want More Link Juice? Here's an Easy Way to Get It'
http://www.wordstream.com/blog/ws/2010/07/15/how-to-find-and-drain-link-juice

[162] Marrs, Megan (November 15, 2016) 'Follow Links vs No Follow Links: Should You Care?' http://www.wordstream.com/blog/ws/2013/07/24/follow-nofollow-links

[163] Patel, Neil (Retrieved March 15, 2017) 'The Seven Commandments of Internal Linking' https://blog.kissmetrics.com/commandments-of-internal-linking/

[164] Hochman, Jonathan (November 24, 2015) 'External Links and SEO' https://www.hochmanconsultants.com/external-links-seo/

[165] Anderson, Shaun (February 3, 2017) 'How to Optimize a Website Structure with Internal Links' http://www.hobo-web.co.uk/optimize-website-navigation/

[166] Crestodina, Andy (Retrieved on February 14, 2017) '3 Internal Linking Strategies for SEO and Conversions'

https://www.orbitmedia.com/blog/internal-linking/

[167] Meyers, Peter (February 22, 2012) 'The 2 User Metrics That Matter for SEO' https://moz.com/blog/the-2-user-metrics-that-matter-for-seo

[168] Smith, Jarrod (January 11, 2016) 'What Bounce Rate Means for Your SEO Strategy' https://www.seohermit.com/articles/what-bounce-rate-means-for-your-seo-strategy/

[169] Peyton, Jay (February 25, 2014) 'What is the Average Bounce Rate for a Website?' http://www.gorocketfuel.com/the-rocket-blog/whats-the-average-bounce-rate-in-google-analytics/

[170] Saleh, Khalid (Retrieved February 13, 2017) 'How to Split Test Without Harming Your Site's SEO' http://www.invespcro.com/blog/how-to-split-test-without-harming-your-sites-seo/

[171] Patel, Neil (June 11, 2014) 'Understanding the Impact of Dwell Time on SEO' https://www.searchenginejournal.com/understanding-impact-dwell-time-seo/108905/

[172] Patel, Neil (Retrieved February 14, 2017) '13 Ways to Reduce Bounce Rate and Increase Your Conversions' http://neilpatel.com/blog/13-ways-to-reduce-bounce-rate-and-increase-your-conversions/

[173] Shaver, Kelli (February 2, 2012) '7 Ways to Lower Your Website's Bounce Rate' http://mashable.com/2012/02/02/lower-bounce-rate-tips/

[174] Anthony (January 31, 2012) 'Why External Links Should Open in New Tabs' http://uxmovement.com/navigation/why-external-links-should-open-in-new-tabs/

[175] Friedman, Vitaly (July 31, 2008) 'Should Links Open in New Windows?' https://www.smashingmagazine.com/2008/07/should-links-open-in-new-windows/

[176] Aragon, Kathryn (Retrieved February 13, 2017) 'The Essence of SEO: What Is High Quality Content?' https://www.crazyegg.com/blog/what-is-high-quality-content/

[177] Hall, Joe (January 23, 2014) 'Do Not Build High Quality for SEO, Build High Quality Patterns Instead' https://www.internetmarketingninjas.com/blog/search-engine-optimization/build-high-quality-content-seo-build-high-quality-patterns-instead/

[178] Patel, Neil (Retrieved February 16, 2017) 'How to Write Content for People and Optimize for Google' http://neilpatel.com/blog/seo-copywriting-how-to-write-content-for-people-and-optimize-for-google-2/

[179] DeMers, Jayson (August 25, 2014) 'The 12 Essential Elements of High Quality Content' https://www.forbes.com/sites/jaysondemers/2014/08/25/the-12-essential-elements-of-high-quality-content/#165749fa533c

[180] Dias, Nelson (August 7, 2016) '55 SEO Copywriting Tips for Rocking Content' http://writtent.com/blog/35-seo-copywriting-tips-rocking-content/

[181] Bigby, Garenne (October 31, 2016) '13 Avoidable Content Mistakes That Can Harm Your SEO' https://dynomapper.com/blog/21-sitemaps-and-seo/244-13-avoidable-content-mistakes-that-can-harm-your-seo

[182] Lloyd-Martin, Heather (March 17, 2016) 'What Is SEO Copywriting and Why Is It Important?' http://seocopywriting.com/what-is-seo-copywriting-and-why-is-it-important-to-my-site/

[183] Clark, Brian (February 3, 2010) 'Does SEO Copywriting Still Matter?' http://www.copyblogger.com/seo-copywriting-matter/

[184] Brooke, Justin (Retrieved February 16, 2017) 'The 20% of SEO That Creates 80% of the Results' https://medium.com/justinbrooke/the-20-of-seo-that-creates-80-of-the-results-3477fbb57c8b#.pkfb66nmn

[185] Jafri, Salma (January 27, 2014) 'How to Write Headlines Google Will Love' https://searchenginewatch.com/sew/how-to/2325076/how-to-write-headlines-google-will-love-you-and-i-will-click-read-and-share

[186] Halbrooks, Glenn (October 17, 2016) 'How to Create SEO Headlines That Will Get Clicks' https://www.thebalance.com/how-to-create-seo-headlines-that-will-get-clicks-2315320

[187] Moon, Garrett (January 20, 2017) 'How to Write Emotional Headlines That Get More Shares' https://coschedule.com/blog/emotional-headlines/

[188] Ellering, Nathan (June 20, 2016) 'How to Write Headlines That Drive, Traffic, Shares, and Search Results' https://coschedule.com/blog/how-to-write-the-best-headlines-that-will-increase-traffic/

[189] DeGeyter, Stoney (May 7, 2012) 'How to Use Customer Personalities to Write Effective SEO Content' https://www.searchenginejournal.com/how-to-use-customer-personalities-to-write-effective-seo-content/43345/

[190] Havice, Jennifer (Retrieved February 16, 2017) 'How to Keep the Personality in Your Copy without Losing Conversions' https://blog.bidsketch.com/sales/copywriting-with-personality/

[191] Urban, Diane (January 26, 2011) '9 Ways to Encourage People to Comment on Your Blog' https://blog.hubspot.com/blog/tabid/6307/bid/8906/9-Ways-to-Encourage-People-to-Comment-on-your-Blog.aspx

[192] Burton, Robin (March 14, 2016) '5 reasons Why Fresh Content is Critical for Your Website and SEO' https://seositecheckup.com/articles/5-reasons-why-fresh-content-is-critical-for-your-website-and-seo

[193] Hines, Kristi (Retrieved February 18, 2017) 'How to Get Google to Index Your New Website Quickly' https://blog.kissmetrics.com/get-google-to-index/

[194] Patel, Neil (Retrieved February 18, 2017) '5 Simple Steps That Will Help You Determine How Often You Need to   Blog' http://neilpatel.com/blog/5-simple-steps-thatll-help-you-determine-how-often-you-need-to-blog/

[195] Birch, Dan (January 21, 2017) 'The Future of SEO in 2017: Things You Need to Change Now' http://victoriousseo.com/future-seo-2017-things-need-change-now/

[196] Sena, Peter (February 11, 2015) 'How to Win the SEO and Content Marketing Arms Race' https://blog.hubspot.com/agency/seo-content-marketing-arms-race

[197] Bryan, Derek (September 26, 2016) 'Five Bold Predictions about the Future of SEO and Social Media Marketing' http://www.marketingprofs.com/opinions/2016/30709/five-bold-predictions-about-the-future-of-seo-and-social-media-marketing

[198] Fishkin, Rand (December 4, 2015) 'Mobile Web vs Mobile Apps: Where Should You Invest Your Marketing?' https://moz.com/blog/mobile-web-mobile-apps-invest-marketing-whiteboard-friday

[199] DeMers, Jayson (November 12, 2015) 'What Is Google RankBrain and Why Does It Matter?' https://www.forbes.com/sites/jaysondemers/2015/11/12/what-is-google-rankbrain-and-why-does-it-matter/#773087ab536b

[200] Long, Rory (April 12, 2016) 'How Google is Interpreting Content in 2016' http://www.thedrum.com/opinion/2016/04/12/how-google-interpreting-content-2016

[201] Sullivan, Danny (June 23, 2016) 'All about the Google RankBrain Algorithm' http://searchengineland.com/faq-all-about-the-new-google-rankbrain-algorithm-234440

[202] Marrs, Megan (April 3, 2015) 'Predictive Search: Is the Future or End of Search?' http://www.wordstream.com/blog/ws/2013/06/24/predictive-search

[203] Laskowski, Nicole (October 10, 2011)' Predictive Analytics and Big Data; The Good, the Bad and the Ugly' http://searchbusinessanalytics.techtarget.com/news/224010 0743/Predictive-analytics-and-big-data-The-good-the-bad-and-the-ugly

[204] Smith, Chris (August 11, 2014) 'Using Autocomplete to Hijack Local Search Results and Improve Online Reputation' http://searchengineland.com/using-autocomplete-hijack-local-search-results-improve-online-reputation-199568

[205] McMgee, Matt (June 20, 2011) '21 Essential SEO Tips and Techniques' http://searchengineland.com/21-essential-seo-tips-techniques-11580

[206] Critchlow, Will (December 7, 2015) 'SEO Split Testing: How to A/B Test Changes for Google' https://moz.com/blog/seo-split-testing-a-b-test-changes-google

[207] Parsons, Noah (Retrieved February 18, 2017) 'The 6 Most Important Web Metrics to Track for Your Business Website' http://articles.bplans.com/the-6-most-important-web-metrics-to-track-for-your-business-website/

[208] Patel, Neil (July 20, 2015) 'The 14 Most Important SEO Metrics' https://www.quicksprout.com/2015/07/20/quantify-your-results-the-14-most-important-seo-metrics/

[209] Sculthorp, Christian (January 24, 2017) '9 Critical SEO Metrics Your Agency Needs to Track' https://agencyanalytics.com/blog/seo-metrics

[210] Teixeira, Joe (May 25, 2011) 'Entrances, Bounces, and Exits: What Does It All Mean?' http://www.morevisibility.com/blogs/analytics/entrances-bounces-and-exits-what-does-it-all-mean.html

[211] Komack, Andy (March 2, 2011) '10 Quick and Dirty SEO Success Metrics' http://searchengineland.com/10-quick-dirty-seo-success-metrics-65842

[212] Jackson, Mark (October 7, 2013) 'Sitemaps and SEO: An Introductory Guide' https://searchenginewatch.com/sew/how-to/2048706/the-site-map-gateway-optimization